Songa's Story

Songa's Story

✳

How A Shtetl Jew Found the American Dream

Natalie Green Giles
with
Betty Ajces

iUniverse, Inc.
New York Lincoln Shanghai

Songa's Story
How A Shtetl Jew Found the American Dream

iUniverse, Inc.

For information address:
iUniverse, Inc.
2021 Pine Lake Road, Suite 100
Lincoln, NE 68512
www.iuniverse.com

ISBN: 0-595-27516-8 (pbk)
ISBN: 0-595-65683-8 (cloth)

Printed in the United States of America

Contents

Preface

I often did not understand my Uncle Leon when he talked. The husband of my father's sister, Betty, his voice was gravelly, and he spoke English through a thick Russian accent. He once led the wife of his business partner through a cocktail party, pointing out to her all of the guests whom he considered to be his "very close friends." His partner's wife only heard, however, that the party was attended by an unusually large number of people with "varicose veins."

Leon could easily and impatiently dismiss you as an *idiot*, or more likely, a *schlemiel*, if you didn't understand what he said, or for that matter, agree with what he said. "You know what I would do," he would often say when referring to an individual or an entire population that espoused an ideology or behaved in a way inconsistent with his own beliefs, "I would put them up against the wall and shoot them." Coming of age under Stalin's totalitarian regime had left its mark. Patience and tolerance were not in his repertoire of instinctive traits.

By the time I was born, Leon was almost fifty years old, and he had already witnessed, participated in, and survived some of the greatest events and atrocities in modern history. I knew that I could never understand this complex man. I was a young American, reared in relatively peaceful and prosperous times, in a country where democracy and freedom are considered an entitlement. I could never comprehend the impact of the social, political, and economic forces that shaped who he was and how he viewed the world. I only vaguely understood that men and women like him had lived through a time in history when chaos and evil prevailed—and might even have triumphed had it not been for their sacrifices and heroic efforts.

I wanted to know more. I was always drawn to a long hallway leading to the study of his well-appointed Long Island home, the only spot in the enormous house where Leon displayed tangible clues to understanding his past. The wall was lined with framed photographs and other memorabilia: aged but well-preserved pictures, medals, and certificates with Polish writing, stamped with official seals. I would stare intently at the photographs of Leon, intimidated by his appearance in full military regalia, stars and medals everywhere, and at the time, a high ranking Jewish officer in Stalin's Communist Polish Army.

Next to these imposing pictures hung the softer, gentler faces of his parents, sister, and brother, ghosts now, whose lives were brutally and prematurely ended. I had only heard pieces of stories about this intensely private man's life. They had always been in hushed words, fragments about murdered parents, horrors of war, surviving Soviet political prison, defection, even divulging military secrets to the Pentagon. I tried to use this wall of remembrance to fit the pieces together. I never dared to ask questions.

He told tales of his past all of the time, but the stories were mere snippets presented for entertainment value—like how he and his fellow soldiers made moonshine vodka out of potatoes in the Eastern front battlefields of World War II. "Hey, Chaim Yankel," he would call out to me, referring to me as the Yiddish equivalent of John Doe—despite my gender—his unique way of inviting me to sit and talk with him. Leon loved to hold court, becoming more and more animated as we silently hung onto his every word. He was history, not the way we learned it in school, but live, three-dimensional history. He never painted the real picture of what he had been through; he never spun his stories into morality tales.

Everyone who heard his stories was transfixed. His past was so incongruent with his present, where he lived the American dream in the lap of Long Island luxury. As he heartily consumed iced cold vodka by his obsessively clean swimming pool on splendid summer afternoons, proudly serving his prized home-grown tomatoes with child-like enthusiasm (they were, to be fair, the best tomatoes anyone had ever tasted), one could not imagine that this was the same man, who starving and exhausted, plucked and hungrily devoured raw onions from the Ukrainian fields as he marched in hurried retreat from Nazi invaders.

Throughout his later years, people encouraged him to formally record his remarkable story. While modest by nature, he was intrigued with the idea, but never made it a priority. And as he became increasingly ill from the lung cancer that eventually took his life, he chose to channel his dwindling energy into a continuous shock and disbelief in his own mortality, to the detriment of attempting to preserve his past, and perhaps achieve some form of immortality. For a man who lived the first eighty years of life without so much as a headache, a man who never took a pill—not even an aspirin—for most of his life, falling gravely ill was an affront to his sense of being. This man, who had escaped the death warrants of Hitler, Stalin, and later, the Mafia, had lost his instinct and desire to fight. Retreating deeper and deeper into his own inner turmoil, he lost interest in sharing his story with the world at large.

Leon's widow, Betty, and I felt compelled to provide a posthumous testimonial to his extraordinary life. Some of the details have been lost forever, but for the most part, his stories have lived on through all of the people who were close to him, particularly through Betty and her astoundingly robust trove of vivid, detailed memories, shared by her husband over the course of forty-two years of marriage.

Songa's Story is a story of survival outside the familiar narrative of Holocaust survival. It is a story whose telling would have invited imprisonment, or even death, as recently as 15 years ago, had it been told by Leon himself, in his native country. It is a story of remarkable perseverance, reinvention, luck, and above all, improbable success attained through one man's raw need to achieve.

Introduction

Almost one million Jewish soldiers fought in the Red Army and the Polish Army forces in the Eastern European battlefields of World War II. These men were not the *Greatest Generation* heroes now immortalized in print and film. These men were not fighting for the preservation of democracy. They, regardless of their individual beliefs, fought Stalin's ideological war of Communism against the Fascists. As Red Army and Polish Army soldiers, they were subject to the ruthless tactics of a dictator who ruled through fear and paranoia, having no regard for their individual humanity, and who shamelessly violated their human rights.

And for those lucky few who survived and claimed victory over the Nazis in World War II, they returned home, not to parades and joyous celebrations, but to desecrated and destroyed hometowns, murdered families, and often stinging anti-Semitic sentiments from non-Jewish survivors in their home villages. Songa was one of these *lucky* survivors.

This book honors these uncelebrated heroes—particularly those few who are still alive to bear witness, but whose numbers diminish daily—and seeks to preserve their place in history.

Prologue: 1944

Songa had become accustomed to counting the passage of time in days; he had learned not to presume survival more than a day at a time. He was quick with numbers. As he sped on horseback toward Ozeryany, the village he had once called home, he made the calculation: one thousand five hundred and ninety days had passed since the day he left. It didn't seem possible. His mind wandered as the horse's hooves pounded along the ground, bringing him closer and closer to Ozeryany. Somehow, the elapsed time seemed to melt away. Somehow, Songa found himself able to put aside the sights and sounds of war that played continuously in his head, just long enough to vividly reconstruct the memory of the last encounter with his family.

It was in the fall of 1939. He was standing on the platform of the train station, looking into his father's eyes. He felt that he still had much to prove to this man who had always expected so much of him. "You will be proud of me," Songa thought to himself. As the whistle blew, the twenty-three-year-old Songa, Polish citizen until the Soviets took control of his village only weeks before, hurried to board the train headed for the Red Army training camp. Soon he would be an enlisted soldier in the Soviet army.

It all seemed surreal. He was leaving behind his home, his identity, his aspirations, and his ideologies. Songa looked once more at his family as he climbed onto the train, instantly regretting the moment: he had caught a glimpse of his father's face. It wasn't the usual confident and self-assured expression that his father wore. It was a terrible expression that Songa had never been allowed to see—a face of uncertainty. It was a fearful face.

Songa hesitantly sat down in his seat as the train slowly pulled away from the station. He had to replace that mental snapshot. He stumbled a bit as he twisted and strained his neck to catch another glimpse of his family, still congregated on the platform. He had missed his chance. Within an instant, their faces were out of view. The people he loved had become nothing more than outlines—featureless and indistinguishable from the other human forms huddled on the platform. With no other choice, Songa turned and settled into his seat. He quietly watched the landscape slip by, the golden grain fields and fruit orchards of his hometown of Ozeryany, now cast in the dark shadows of Soviet occupation, bracing against the rumblings of encroaching war.

Now, five years later, he coaxed the horse to move faster, wondering how he could still be alive. Here he was, the returning hero, a Jew from a shtetl in western Ukraine, liberator of tens of thousands of people from Nazi occupation, leader of thousands of men who battled against the murderers of millions. Songa allowed himself to imagine the reunion with his parents: how they would look when they saw his officer's uniform, resplendent with medals and decorations of honor, silently testifying to his ample accomplishments. No words would be necessary. Songa knew this time he would finally gain his father's approval.

The war was far from over, but as Songa rode closer and closer to home, the Germans were rapidly retreating, and the Red Army was moving westward, swiftly and decisively. They had recently pushed across the Polish border and could celebrate the complete liberation and reclamation of the Soviet Union. It was the fall of 1944. An unthinkable twenty million Russian soldiers and civilians had died since the start of the war. Yet Songa was alive, more alive today than any other since the German invasion of the Soviet Union. He actually allowed his frozen emotions to thaw, just a bit, as he made his way home.

He remained resolute in his belief that his family would be waiting for him. If he had managed to emerge intact from some of the most ferocious fighting of the war, then his family, too, would have found a way to survive. His will to live had been perpetually fueled by the image he had conjured of the day he would once again hold his mother and father—of the day he would ride into Ozeryany, and perhaps even be the one to heroically liberate his entire family from the murderous claws of the Nazi occupiers. Until that day arrived, someone would have protected a family such as his, so respected and admired in the community. He felt sure of it, even if he had to continuously deny the ample evidence that suggested otherwise.

Over the course of the past five years, Songa had borne witness to the extent of the Nazi destruction. He had come face-to-face with unprecedented evil. He had been among the first troops to discover the concentration camps and crematoriums used to systematically carry out the annihilation of the Jews of Europe. He had seen the devastation and desecration of the Soviet land, villages, and cities as the Red Army pushed the Germans westward. He had heard the stories of the Nazi atrocities from the surviving residents, the accounts of roundups and mass murders of the Jews, the barbaric behavior of the soldiers, the sentiment that the Soviet civilians, and worse, the Soviet Jews, were something less than human. Of course, this could not happen to his family. His story, so far, had been different. Their story, too, would be different.

1

Childhood:
In the Eye of the Storm

He was officially named Lazar, after his maternal grandfather, whose appendix had burst only months before Songa's birth. His mother, still in shock and deeply mourning her father's unexpected death, found it too painful to speak the name out loud, even as she looked into the large, dark eyes of her infant son. "Songa," she began calling her baby. The name had no meaning. It was nothing more than a sound made by a protective young mother as she held her lifeline in her hands. The name comforted her. It was a sound of innocence in the midst of turbulent times. It would remain his name through war and peace, destruction and rebuilding, poverty and prosperity.

It was in the tiny village of Ozeryany in July of 1916 that Songa entered the world. Ozeryany was one of the many Eastern European shtetls, small Jewish villages, in the western portion of the Russian empire in what today is Ukraine. This rural dot on the map was a close-knit community. The hundred or so Jewish families who made up the majority of the population managed to coexist peacefully with the Ukrainian, Polish, and Czech families, all bound by strong economic ties, but maintaining limited social and cultural contact. The Jews in the village enjoyed particularly good camaraderie with all of the populations of non-Jews, ironically acting as the buffer between the Ukrainians and the Poles, who had inherited a tradition of mutual dislike. All of the residents of Ozeryany shared one common bond: they had all migrated to the area because they were drawn to the unparalleled natural abundance produced by the fertile fields of this part of Ukraine—Volhynia—known worldwide as the *breadbasket* of Europe.

Located halfway between the larger Ukrainian cities of Dubno and Rovno, the small village of Ozeryany was graced with natural beauty. Lakes, streams, and densely forested land surrounded the bountiful grain farms and fruit orchards. The Jews were not farmers, but agriculture provided the basis of their commerce. They brought their skills as grain merchants, cattle dealers, craftsmen, and tradesmen to the region. The abundance of grain also produced a thriving spirits business, and Jewish families took over the production and distillery of alcohol and whiskey, an unlikely but profitable initiative for what some have called "the most sober" of cultures.

However, the pastoral setting and timeless occupations belied the political events that were threatening to engulf the simple life of the villagers. As Songa entered the world, the Russian empire, under Tsar Nicholas II, was drawing its last breath after nearly three hundred years of Romanov rule. The Communist Bolsheviks prepared for their bloody revolution, aided by the chaos and distraction of a world at war. The changing political and ideological upheaval was poised to radically transform the region for most of the twentieth century. And yet, life went on.

Ozeryany was little more than one unpaved main street, far removed from both the bustle, as well as the modern conveniences of city living. People traveled by horse and carriage on dirt roads. Houses had no indoor plumbing. Only the wealthiest few families had a telephone. Bicycles were a symbol of modernity and a popular means of transportation. However, as seemingly isolated and provincial as it was, Ozeryany did have a train station, which happened to fall right on the main line for the railroad to Kiev, the cultural and intellectual capital of Ukraine.

It was the existence of the train station that enabled the chance meeting of Melech Ajces (pronounced *Aitzes*), an educated and cosmopolitan young man from the city, and the beautiful Yetta Feinblatt, a young country girl whose family had been in Ozeryany for many generations. The story goes that young Melech was passing through Ozeryany on the train, on the way to visit his relatives. When he got out at the train station, he laid eyes on Yetta, standing on the platform, and fell instantly in love with her. He was so determined to be with this woman that he hastily abandoned his ambitious plans, and decided to leave his worldly, educated life behind. Melech was *Russified,* the kind of assimilated Jew who did not practice religion, and whose identity was very much defined by Russian culture, language, literature, and music. Melech spoke Russian at home; Yetta spoke Yiddish. It was much to the dismay of Melech's parents and twin brother that he chose the provincial, unsophisticated shtetl life as the place where he would live and raise his family. They married in 1910. Melech was twenty-five and Yetta was twenty-two.

As the oldest of eight children, Yetta held a special responsibility as the family caretaker. Melech and Yetta began their married life in the comfortably large house of Yetta's childhood, living alongside all of the immediate Feinblatt family members, including her parents, Miriam and Lazar, with whom Yetta was exceptionally close.

Yetta had little formal education, though she had learned to read and write, surpassing the skills of her mother, Miriam, who remained illiterate throughout her life. Making up for her lack of formal academic training, Yetta was graced with enviable innate business acumen. It was generally acknowledged that she could sell just about anything to anyone. For the most part, women did not work outside the home in the village, but Yetta felt compelled to employ her talents as an entrepreneur. She took advantage of the thriving local spirits business, by running a tavern in the village. For a rural Jewish girl, whose family saved the drinking for the important holidays, serving alcohol to the local men was an unusual pursuit, and one that met its share of disapproval from other Jewish women in a village where gossiping was a favorite pastime.

While Yetta was exercising her head for business, Melech employed his training as a medical assistant. Ozeryany was a town with only one doctor, and Melech often stepped in to perform the routine medical procedures for the villagers. Eventually, Melech's advanced education and training propelled him into the informal role of wise man to the Jews in the village. He became the trusted adviser to whom the Jews would turn for guidance and direction on a variety of secular issues. Melech's position was quite an important one in the shtetl, and brought with it high social standing for the family in the Jewish community.

By 1913, the young Ajces family had grown, with the birth of Yetta and Melech's first child, a baby girl they named Rose. Three years later, on July 15, 1916, Songa was born. Only one year later, the Bolsheviks overthrew the Tsar and seized control of Russia. The following year, the Germans surrendered. After four years of the bloodiest warfare the modern world had ever witnessed, World War I ended.

As a new world order took hold, in the wake of the end of the war, the villagers of Ozeryany were informed of their fate. Within just three short years, Ozeryany had passed hands from the Russian Empire, to the Soviet revolutionaries, to a now newly independent Poland. As a result of the redrawing of European borders, based on agreements outlined in the Treaty of Versailles, Poland emerged as one of the winners of World War I. For the first time in over one hundred years, Poland regained territory lost decades earlier to the Russian Empire. Poland was restored to independent nation status, and the Second Republic of Poland was created. Melech and Yetta Ajces, and their entire family, reared as Jewish citizens of the Russian Empire, who fearfully witnessed the Bolshevik revolution, were now under Polish rather than Communist rule. Immediately, the official language of their region changed from Russian to Polish.

Through a stroke of the pen that enacted the Treaty of Versailles, Songa and his family were to remain a part of the capitalist West, spared the major social and economic changes of their new Communist neighbor only miles to the east. While the citizens of the Soviet Union were subjected to the new repressive ways of a state-owned, and state-run world, the newly formed republic of Poland allowed people to go about their business. The Poles were fairly hands-off in their governing when it came to their Eastern territory. The villagers in Ozeryany could continue to conduct their commerce, practice their religions, receive *western* educations, and live their lives according to their own, personal ideologies. They felt that they had their freedom.

Songa was only three years old by the time all of the tumult had settled, and the ensuing twenty years of *interwar* Polish rule provided a remarkably peaceful and stable backdrop for a simple, happy, and nurturing childhood. His childhood was an aberration, a cozy interlude between two catastrophic world wars. It coincided with an eerily quiet *eye* in an apocalyptic political storm that blanketed Europe during most of the first half of the twentieth century. The storm would, of course, resume its devastation in the not too distant future, but Songa was given the chance to grow up.

With the birth of a third child in 1919, named Josef, the Ajces family was complete. The house was now full, with the three children surrounded by aunts, uncles, grandmother, and great-grandfather, the extended family, all of whom shared the large, comfortable home. The house was enormous, even by American standards. Songa's grandmother, Miriam, presided over the kitchen, and insisted on doing all of the cooking for the entire family. Wonderful aromas of the continuous meal preparation always filled the house.

The door to the Ajces home was always open to visitors. A pot of tea, and bread with jam were at the ready, to be offered to women in the parlor, as their husbands arrived to consult with Melech, the counselor, in the study. Music resonated throughout the house. The sounds of a mandolin, or a balalaika, and accompanying voices singing Russian, Jewish, and Ukrainian folk songs, punctuated the everyday banter of Yiddish, Russian, Polish, and Hebrew that constantly filled their home. The natural beauty of the Ukraine's Volhyene region provided endless entertainment for the children: hiking, climbing trees in the fruit orchards, swimming in the lake behind the house, and ice skating in the winter. It was a perfect childhood.

The simplicity and quiet elegance of the reasonably wealthy, well-respected family's lifestyle afforded Songa every opportunity to thrive, despite the fact that he was a sickly child. Painfully thin, and prone to illness in his early childhood, he became the center of attention, particularly of his mother, grandmother, and his aunts. The doting and fussing over their *Songale* became an unbreakable habit, even after he had overcome the childhood illnesses. In their eyes, Songa could do no wrong.

In addition to his good looks, everything came naturally to Songa. He excelled as an athlete, a scholar, and a musician. But, he had an impish personality, and delighted in benign mischief. Songa soon became known as the *bandit*. He was always playing tricks and challenging the rules. He charmed his grandmother into becoming a co-conspirator by helping him sneak out of the house at night through open windows; she would always make sure a window remained open for his undetected return. Songa's favorite target was his neighbor, Moishe Yankel, the farmer who owned the apple orchard just behind Songa's house.

Songa loved to infuriate Moishe Yankel, who was very protective of his orchards, by sneaking over the fence, and climbing into the trees to eat the apples. "I know you are up there, you thief," Moishe Yankel would cry out, shaking his fist as Songa sat high in the trees, eating the apples until his stomach began to ache. For Songa, the discomfort of a stomach ache was only a small price for the mischievous pleasure he got as he always managed to elude the angry farmer and escape safely back to his own house.

Songa's carefree spirit and natural talent was overshadowed by Melech's exceedingly high expectations for his first son. Unlike most of the shtetl's residents, Melech was extremely well educated. He had the highest aspirations for his son, and he saw education as the only route to successfully achieve those aspirations. Since they were a family of means, Melech chose to school Songa at home for his early education, providing him with private tutors until he was thirteen years old. In the village, private tutors were seen as the preferable alternative for the wealthier, educated, and more progressive Jews. Songa was rigorously tutored in all of the traditional academic subjects, in Russian and Hebrew, as well as in Jewish study.

Despite the fact that Songa undertook formal Jewish studies, the family was not observant of, nor did they practice Judaism in their home. Unlike many of their neighbors, most of which were very religious, the Ajces family did not keep a kosher home, nor did they observe the Sabbath rituals. There were three synagogues in Ozeryany, and rarely did the family attend. Culturally however, they felt very strong ties to their Jewish identity, and as secular Jews, they became swept up in the Zionist movement.

Three of Songa's aunts and uncles made their way to Palestine in the early 1930's as part of the Zionist effort to create a Jewish homeland. Songa, as a teenager, was an avid member of the Betar, one of several Zionist youth groups dedicated to establishing a homeland for Jews dispersed around the world. Betar intended to provide identification with Israel for young people, but unlike other Zionist movements, it was rooted in a conservative, militaristic approach to achieving its goals. Betar created the Jewish self-defense unit, teaching Jews to protect themselves from oppressors by force of arms.

It was the politics and teaching of Betar's Russian founder, Vladimir Zhabotinsky that particularly captured Songa's imagination. He began envisioning that one day, he, too, would settle in Palestine, joining the effort to reclaim Israel for the Jewish people. While he himself had never experienced the forces of oppression and anti-Semitism that Betar's charismatic leader spoke of, he knew full well the suffering of Jews in the intensely anti-Semitic Polish areas close to his home. Songa found the notion of self-defense, of struggling to end oppression as an armed fighter, very appealing.

He quickly distinguished himself as a bright and able student, particularly compared to his younger brother, and chief rival, Josef. Josef, blessed with the good looks of a matinee-idol, was always more distracted by physical pleasures, to the detriment of his studies. Songa was soon recognized as the *brain* of the family. Josef, in contrast, was slotted into the role of the fun-loving party boy. Expectations for Josef were transferred to Songa. And still, despite Songa's scholastic success, he began to believe he could never reach the levels of achievement necessary to satisfy his very demanding father. The more Songa achieved, the higher Melech set the bar for achievement. Melech believed Songa's studies should take precedence over all else, and would chastise him, if, for example, he should be so *frivolous* as to go out and play soccer rather than study. "You'll never amount to anything," Melech would often say.

But Melech recognized his son's exceptional talents. He was simply relentless in his insistence that Songa make the most of his ability, perhaps frustrated by his own life choices that left his considerable talents underutilized. Songa's perception that he was unable to meet his father's expectations would haunt him for years to come.

By 1925, the picture of the idyllic childhood days began to change. On the cusp of her adolescence, Songa's sister Rose suddenly began to behave erratically. She seemed to be suffering from a mental breakdown, showing signs of mental instability. With such scarce medical resources in the tiny village of Ozeryany, and even in the neighboring larger village of Warkowicze, Yetta and Melech found themselves in the throes of trying to find doctors who could help Rose.

Between the trips to various nearby cities, and the medical expenses themselves, Rose's illness came at a great cost to the family, both financially, and emotionally. Suddenly, Yetta was not there for her two younger sons, always off to a new doctor in the hopes of finding a cure for her daughter. Eventually, they gave up, now poor and emotionally drained, and resigned themselves to a life with a mentally disabled daughter. Much of the burden for looking after Rose fell on Songa's

Aunt Ruchel, the youngest of Yetta's seven siblings. Yet, despite the continued outpouring of love and attention from his grandmother, aunts, and uncles, Songa and Josef were deeply affected by Rose's illness and the stress it put on their parents. Songa watched helplessly as his once beautiful and vibrant mother grew old prematurely.

The Ajces family's world continued to crumble a few years later. By 1929, their resources were depleted in the quest to cure Rose. While the world suffered the ramifications of the U.S. stock market crash, Songa's family faced their own economic devastation. Their money was gone. They were poor. They became dependent on the fertile Ukrainian farmland, and began to grow their own crops as their primary food source. In addition, Melech's parents, who had played a relatively insignificant role in Songa's life to date, became increasingly important. Songa's paternal grandparents, along with his father's twin brother, had been living in England for some time, and managed to send packages of goods and money back to the family in Ozeryany. Melech's father went so far as to visit his son and daughter-in-law in Ozeryany, pleading with them to pack up and move to England. But Yetta would not leave her mother. The younger Ajces family remained in Ozeryany, and Songa's grandfather returned to England, alone, a decision that would separate them forever.

Songa turned thirteen and Melech was unable to continue to support the costs of home tutors. He decided that Songa would not go to a Jewish school, like most of the shtetl's Jewish population, but to gymnasium, a Polish school, where he would get a proper Polish education. The Jewish schools were not officially accredited by the Polish government, and therefore, were not considered feeder schools to the universities. The Jewish schools conducted classes primarily in Yiddish. Melech would have no part of that. Instead he sent his son to the only Polish gymnasium that would accept him as a Jew, a school in the town of Brode, located about seventy kilometers from Ozeryany. Young Songa would be leaving home for the first time.

To leave the cloistered comfort of his shtetl was a life-altering move for Songa. The journey to Brode, seventy kilometers on unpaved roads, riding in a horse drawn carriage, took almost a full day. But more than the physical distance would be the psychological distance. He would leave the close-knit Jewish community of Ozeryany to become one of only two Jewish students in the Polish school. For the first time in his young life, Songa would be forced to confront the fact that he was different. He would be forced to understand what it meant to be a Jew in a notoriously anti-Semitic country.

Despite the strangeness of it all, Songa assimilated immediately, and excelled academically and socially in Brode. He spent only three years there, however, because Melech had arranged for Songa to transfer to a more prestigious gymnasium in Warsaw.

Warsaw was known as the "Paris of the East," and the cultural Mecca was magnificent to the eyes of the country boy from Ozeryany. The only cities Songa had seen up to that point, Dubno and Rovno, were mere villages compared to bustling Warsaw. He soaked in the cosmopolitan atmosphere, basking in the intellectual energy that permeated the city. Here, Songa's course of studies became increasingly rigorous, including the very Western study of classical Latin and Greek. He was preparing himself for a university education. If he succeeded, he would be the first person from the town of Ozeryany to attend university.

Melech had arranged for Songa to stay in Warsaw with a distant relative who was an extremely wealthy woman. She lived in a beautiful home, replete with all of the trappings of the urban wealthy. Songa had never seen such a home before. When the teenage boy from the farm country arrived at her house, the butler greeted him at the door with a tray on which he was to lay his calling card. Songa, completely unaware of the rituals, replied that he had no card. The butler allowed him to enter the house anyway, and brought him to the drawing room to introduce him to the lady of the house. Songa did not know that her extended hand was to be kissed upon introduction. The woman withdrew her hand silently and said nothing of it at the time. But Songa was never invited back to the house.

When Melech learned of his son's breach of manners, he was furious. Songa could not understand his father's fury. "All this because I didn't kiss her hand?" He quickly became disgusted by the unwritten rules of the rich. He was unimpressed by the required customs and ceremonial airs. He was a hard working boy from the shtetl, and would never pretend to be anything other than who he was.

While he failed in his attempt to impress the wealthy woman of Warsaw, Songa had significantly greater success with the women back home in Ozeryany. Handsome, with his olive complexion and dark eyes, strong, smart, and full of life, Songa was quite a catch for the Jewish girls of Ozeryany. He, unlike his brother, was always respectful of girls. Josef was known as a *lady-killer*, who was likely to chase anything in a skirt.

Josef, much to the embarrassment of his parents, had many affairs, and not always with the appropriate partners. Melech became quite disturbed with Josef's growing reputation. Songa, in contrast, was more discriminating in his selection of girlfriends. Both boys liked to proclaim their link to the strong virility genes of their maternal great-grandfather, who at the grand age of ninety-six, came home one day and proclaimed to his daughter, Songa's grandmother, Miriam, that within the year he would marry the village's twenty-eight year-old school teacher and have a child with her. Apparently there was a legitimate attraction between the two; however, a real romance never had the chance to materialize. Songa's great-grandfather died peacefully shortly after his proclamation.

Songa was finally caught, by one of his many admirers in the town. Her name was Rosa Spitzkopf, and she would have the distinction of becoming his first serious girlfriend. Ironically, with all of his choices, Songa described Rosa as a relatively homely girl. Most boys Songa's age operated on a much more superficial level when it came to their love interests, but what attracted Songa to her was her musical ability.

Rosa was an extremely talented pianist who connected with Songa in their mutual love of music. Their relationship was undone, however, when they both applied to the prestigious Conservatory of Music, he on the mandolin and she on the piano. The confident Songa, for whom things came so naturally and easily, was accepted to the Conservatory while Rosa was not. She had dedicated countless hours to study; he had never studied music formally.

It was in the summer of 1933, that Songa unleashed the capitalist within him. Watching his mother run the tavern all those years had inspired him to start a business of his own. With the cocky confidence of a well-educated seventeen-year-old, Songa—completely non-mechanical and useless with tools—set out to start a bicycle repair business. He saw a big business opportunity. Everyone had bicycles in this town with no cars. The railroad was the prime mode of transportation for big trips to the cities, but the young people were often known to ride their bikes for up to two hours, to the nearby cities of Dubno and Rovno, to go to the movies or hear a lecture. The unpaved roads were hard on the bikes. Someone had to fix them. So, in a village that had little more than two grocery stores, a couple of butchers, a pharmacy, and a tavern, Songa would add a bicycle business.

He found another local boy, Josef Katz, who worked well with tools, and proposed his idea for a partnership. Josef bought into the idea with the understanding that Songa would be the *brains* behind the business, while he performed the manual labor. Despite their partnership status, Songa always viewed himself as the boss.

They rented a storefront space in the heart of Warkowicze, the neighboring village, a few kilometers from Ozeryany. Their landlord, the Trojb family, was a well-respected Jewish family in Warkowicze. The Trojb's twelve-year-old granddaughter, Chana, quickly became infatuated with the dashing and commanding presence of the proprietor of the bicycle shop.

Each morning during that summer, Chana sat at her grandparents' window, anxiously awaiting Songa's arrival. He always arrived at precisely the same time. He always made the same thundering entrance into Warkowicze, speeding in on his motorcycle, and slowly emerging from the cloud of dust kicked up by the motorcycle, to walk the few steps to the bicycle shop. Before entering the store, he would stop to look around, like a feudal lord surveying his lands.

This ritual was always followed by the sound of Songa's booming voice, barking orders for the day, at Josef. At seventeen, Songa had reached his full and unexceptional adult height of five-feet, nine-inches. And yet, he always seemed much taller to those who watched him, his confident, powerful, and controlling ways stretching him out, and making it seem as though he towered over his surroundings.

Just as Songa entered his early twenties, full of boundless energy, and eager to find his place in the world, the long period of peace and relative political stability under Polish rule was starting to waiver. With Hitler's aggressive quest for power in the mid to late 1930s, the Eastern Europeans watched with a cautious eye to see what impact all of this might have on their future.

They heard rumors of the Kristallnacht, the "Night of Broken Glass," in which violent mobs raged through Germany, destroying Jewish businesses, vandalizing schools, and burning synagogues. It all seemed so remote. What would anyone want with them, in their tiny village? Politics took place in the cities. And Songa was restless. He did not want to *wait and see* what the future might bring. He was ready now to explore the world beyond his relatively provincial life in Eastern Europe. Songa resolutely believed those around him who gave little credence to the idea that Hitler would move past Germany. "Hair will grow out of this palm if Hitler starts a war," was the popular Yiddish expression that Songa subscribed to. He could not put his life on hold.

In Songa's eyes, nothing embodied the modern world, and all of the things it had to offer, more than the World's Fair that was set to open in 1939, in New York City. He read about the exhibits—advances in technology that seemed impossible to a young man reared in a small village in Ukraine. He read about television, air conditioning, and pavilions where people could use telephones to call people across oceans. Songa wanted to go. He needed to see all of this for himself.

Despite the prevailing sentiments that it was not a good time to travel, it was still early in 1939, and Songa began to make plans for the trip. He managed to convince his beloved Aunt Ziesel to go with him to America. They would see the World's Fair, and visit their family in New York City. By this time, two of Yetta's brothers, Morris and Julius, were already living successful lives in New York, having left Ozeryany in the late 1920s.

Songa dreamed about the trip constantly. He envisioned it as his awakening, an invitation to all of the limitless possibilities that lay before him. But as 1939 progressed, the war seemed to be moving closer and closer to home. Melech and Yetta had lived through war. They could feel the rising undercurrents of uncertainty, and convinced Songa and Ziesel to postpone their travel plans until things settled down. It would, of course, be many, many years, before anything settled down.

2

Songa the Soldier

Hitler invaded Poland on September 1, 1939. As part of his campaign to take over Poland, he had colluded with Stalin to create a so-called non-aggression pact—the Ribbentrop-Molotov pact—that allowed Hitler to begin World War II without fear of a second front opening up in the East.

That pact contained a secret protocol that divided the territory located between Germany and the Soviet Union. Hitler would take his share and hand everything east of the demarcation line to Stalin. Eastern Poland, including Ozeryany, would be taken over by the Soviets. On September 18, with western Poland occupied by German forces, Soviet troops, youthful and enthusiastic, marched into Ozeryany.

The villagers stood in the streets, outside their houses, and watched as the convoy of Soviet trucks, tanks, and horses moved slowly past them. For Songa's family, and the other citizens of Ozeryany, it was not clear who the worst enemy might be: the German soldiers with their rumored but seemingly remote campaign against the Jews, or these Soviet soldiers, with their promise to *liberate* the non-Communist westerners.

Two weeks passed uneventfully; after the drama of the parade of soldiers and munitions, little changed in Ozeryany after the Soviet occupation. The villagers went about their business as they tried to understand the impact of the occupation. But when the Soviet commander arrived, the *sovietization* process began.

It was not going to be business as usual. The villagers began to understand that their simple, peaceful ways would be no more. Their freedoms began to unravel, with simple things at first. Russian soldiers took bicycles away from the children. "What do you need it for?" the soldiers asked the children. "The state will give you everything you need."

Young soldiers were dispatched throughout the town to spread the propaganda, the children being their primary target. "In Russia, you can do anything, and have anything you want." Soon the grocery stores in Ozeryany closed, the shelves empty, with no food to sell. "Everything is coming," the Soviet soldiers reassured them. But nothing ever came.

It was two decades after the revolution, but Songa's parents still referred to the Soviet Communists as the Bolsheviks, and their arrival put the Ajces family and their peers on alert. Anyone who was educated, wealthy, or in any way *elite*, was considered a danger to the Soviet system. As educated people with high standing in the community, living in one of the larger homes in the village, they were easy targets for the rumored purges that had become standard procedure to enforce the Communist doctrine, and weed out potential dissidents. Ruling through fear and terror, the Communists under Stalin often made good on the threat of political prison or exile to labor camps in Siberia.

The more successful villagers in this newly controlled territory, who might be viewed as *too western*, knew they had to keep a low profile. Everyone was to be on equal footing. Everyone had to be poor and miserable now, with goods unavailable, and the currency worthless. Even those few who could still afford to buy material goods, would not, for fear that it would raise suspicion. Often, the Communists used the children as informants against their parents.

Now the villagers were truly conflicted by their fate. They thought about their Polish neighbors to the west, now occupied by the German army. What were they facing in Ozeryany? This was not war. Not a shot had been fired. No one had been taken away—not yet, at least. What if the Germans had gotten to them first? Melech and the other leaders of the Jewish community endlessly debated these questions. Would they be better off under the Germans?

At the time, the villagers believed the Germans were motivated by their quest to achieve more *living space* for the Aryan race and to gain control of Russia's natural resources. No one knew, or could have had the imagination to understand, that the annihilation of the Jewish people was the ultimate goal of the German leader. Nor could these Jews of Ozeryany have imagined that the *godless* Bolshevik Red Army—whose political leaders would strip them of their right to worship—would rise to become the stalwart fighters against the Nazis. No one would have predicted that the soldiers of the Red Army would play such a critical role in the preservation and continuity of Eastern European Jewry.

It was 1939. Melech and his family formulated their opinions based on what evidence they had before them. They feared the Soviet soldiers much more than they feared the Germans, because they had witnessed, firsthand, what the Bolsheviks were capable of doing. They were completely ignorant of the unthinkable villainy that had infected the minds of the Nazi soldiers.

The period of interwar Polish rule was over. The people of Ozeryany were jettisoned back twenty-one years to the days before the end of World War I. Once again, as it was in 1918, life as they knew it was transformed.

The official language of the region reverted back to Russian, and virtually all traces of Polish rule had been eerily erased. Communist doctrine replaced the Polish curriculum taught in the schools. Soviet government offices were set up in all areas, requiring everyone to register for work in support of the Communist Party. All of the farms in this extraordinarily fertile region were now reorganized or *collectivized*, and became state-owned. The practice of religion was forbidden. Fear and paranoia seeped into the carrying out of the most mundane daily activities. Stalin was now their leader.

When the Soviets occupied Eastern Poland, Songa, who had just completed two years of university in the bustling Polish city of Lvov, and was beginning his third, packed up and returned home. Instinctively, he understood that he should leave the university immediately. Suppressing the exchange of ideas in university settings would, in fact, be among Stalin's first orders. Under the Communist regime, the intellectual and aspiring Songa would have to significantly revise his plans for the future. It was Melech who once again took the heavy hand in directing his son's future.

Within weeks of the Communist takeover, Melech calculated what he thought would be the safest and most prudent path for Songa to take: he insisted that Songa enlist as a soldier in Stalin's Red Army. Assimilation is survival, Melech believed.

Songa could not process what his father was suggesting. Here he was, a Zionist Jew, highly educated, with a Polish education, and as anti-Communist as one with a strong, entrepreneurial economic instinct could be. The idea was ludicrous. He would have no part of it. "Don't you understand," Melech said sternly to his son. "For every reason you would have nothing to do with the Red Army…those are exactly the reasons why you must join. There is no other option."

Songa knew his father was right. But he struggled with how he would be able to disguise his contempt for his new role.

At that time, the Red Army was not officially at war. The troops had just taken back the Polish territories from a decisively underpowered Polish Army. The takeover hardly constituted a challenge for the Soviet forces. Stalin's troops literally walked into the eastern Polish cities and villages and proclaimed that they were now in charge. Yet, the brutality the Red Army exhibited against the Polish Army would become a point of contention in Soviet-Polish relations for generations to come.

If the Soviet-Polish politics alone were not enough to suggest that the Red Army offered no compelling call to Songa, consider that this was 1939, and Songa would find himself a soldier in Stalin's army at a time when Stalin was in peaceful collusion with Nazi Germany.

The Soviet Union was busy supplying Germany with food, oil, and raw materials. Remarkably, until 1941, the Soviet Union was considered by Roosevelt and Churchill to be a virtual ally of Nazi Germany. Internal politics cast dark shadows on the legitimacy of the Soviet Army as well.

The Red Army of 1939 was still reeling from Stalin's officer purges in 1937 and 1938. In a fit of paranoid retrofitting, Stalin had ordered the removal of the Army's best and most experienced leaders. Some of the most talented and experienced Russian military leaders were executed or imprisoned. As a result of these ruthless purges, chaos prevailed throughout a relatively inexperienced, undisciplined cadre of Red Army soldiers.

Songa's profound angst and confusion over the decision to enlist would be alleviated shortly. Within weeks after the Soviet occupation, the Red Army began drafting all eligible men in their newly acquired territory. Songa was no longer alone. His brother Josef was soon notified that he had been drafted into a tank corps.

The knowledge that both boys would be away from home—neither of them close by to look after Melech and Yetta in these horribly uncertain times— affected Songa deeply. It would be the first time the family would be so dispersed. They had weathered so much together; their strength was in their closeness.

Songa dreaded his departure for boot camp with a level of anxiety he had never known. He didn't sleep. He could barely eat in the days leading up to his departure. He worked it through over and over in his head; "make it through basic training, do the tour of duty, go home." He kept telling himself that he would be home soon. Then he could figure out with his family what the best course of action might be. "We'll go to Palestine or America. It will all work out."

Songa was the first to leave. Josef would remain in Ozeryany for several more weeks. On the day of his departure, his entire family took him to the train station. He clutched his mother and father at the station in a powerful embrace. He tried to look confident. But as she watched her son leave for basic training, Yetta only saw the thin, sickly little boy he had once been. She wondered how Songa could ever have the strength to survive a war. "Josef is strong," Yetta thought to herself. "He can fight. But Songa will never last."

Once he arrived at training camp, there was little time to think about home. The physical exhaustion of the routine of basic training was all consuming. What energy was left went to the mental adjustment of army life. It quickly became clear that a military life would be a challenge for the fiercely independent and self-assured young man. His slightly mischievous personality, coupled with his strong preference to give, and not receive, orders, proved to be a difficult match with the rigor and unquestioned obedience required in the army. Songa quickly learned the price of disobedience. He performed more than the normal share of latrine cleaning and floor scrubbing, the consequences of deliberately disobeying orders.

In those early days of army life, the temptation to test the limits, usually to go out drinking or enjoy the company of women, outweighed the consequences of breaking the rules. Only now, his doting grandmother was not there to keep the window open for him so that he might sneak back in unnoticed.

As time went on, however, the military indoctrination started to take hold, and Songa actually grew to like, if not thrive on the atmosphere of order, rigor, and discipline that the army imposed. As the drill sergeant shouted, "You have no mother; you have no father; Stalin is your leader and you will fight for Mother Russia," Songa started to believe him. He had great regard for the Red Army as an institution. He found the military mindset, shaped by the authoritative culture and the exacting precision and decisiveness, a comfortable match with his own personality and style. The world through the lens of the Red Army was black or white; there was no gray. Songa's world, too, was becoming increasingly black and white. He had little tolerance for examining different perspectives on issues. If he was given orders, his job was to execute those orders, without asking questions.

The early years of 1939 to 1941 were Songa's formative years as a soldier, as he was shaped and molded into a good soldier. He was on the fast track, rising quickly through the ranks, his intelligence and profound loyalty becoming obvious to all those around him.

He actually enjoyed himself during those early years of infantry training. He liked the camaraderie. He liked the challenge. He liked the uniform. But while Songa grew stronger in body and mind, his family's well being back home in Ozeryany continued to deteriorate under the Soviet regime. Everyone was miserable: Jews, Poles, Ukrainians, it didn't matter who you were. There wasn't enough food. The bare minimum of sustenance was available only because of their proximity to the farms. People in the cities starved. The repressive regime led the villagers to question each other's every move, and to suspiciously eye their neighbors. While Songa found a new community in the army, Ozeryany's spirit of community, once the backbone of shtetl life, had become increasingly fractured.

Songa had very little contact with his family once he left for the army. They wrote letters back and forth, but were limited in what they could say. There was no such thing as privacy under the Soviet system. On two occasions, Yetta was able to take the train to visit her son. The visits were highly anticipated, however, their reunions also underscored the growing divide between them. As much as Songa loved seeing his mother, it upset him that he could not better understand how much things were changing back home. His mother's face wore the visible scars of suffering, fear, and anxiety of an impending war, and there was nothing Songa could do to allay that fear.

3

War

On June 22, 1941, despite Stalin's horribly misguided belief that it would never happen, the Germans betrayed the so-called non-aggression pact and invaded the Soviet Union. The Soviet army was completely blind-sided by the attack, and within weeks, the casualties were catastrophic; two million Red Army soldiers had been killed. The impact of the earlier Communist purges of the Red Army's talented military leaders was clear: Stalin was left with a disorganized and inexperienced force that proved no match for the well-organized German army.

Almost immediately, the Soviet forces were in full retreat as the Germans stormed east. Such was the ease and speed of conquest that Hitler predicted total defeat of the Soviet Union within three months. His intent was the utter and total destruction of Moscow, and everything in its path. The Soviet land, rich in oil and other natural resources, was to be claimed as new territory for German colonization, providing the needed *living space* for the Aryan nation. Hitler's hatred for Bolshevik Communism was second only to his hatred for the Jews. Songa, being a Jew and a Red Army soldier, was holding two death warrants in the eyes of the German invaders.

With the Red Army thrust into total disarray, the institution Songa had come to so admire for its order and rigor had become unrecognizable. The extent of confusion was so great that the Soviet Union went to war without a commander-in-chief. Destruction and chaos on the fronts abounded, and yet, Soviet commanders, under punishing assault, were told to simply "wait" in their positions. Communications networks were decimated. It would be many hours of relentless attack before Songa's division even understood what was happening to them; that they were, in fact, at war.

Completely unprepared for the invasion of their homeland, the Red Army soldiers' daily existence quickly deteriorated. The soldiers had inadequate equipment and supplies, and were completely ill equipped tactically, and psychologically to take on the impressive, well-organized German armies. The Soviets had no choice but to flee eastward in full retreat, abandoning the Western borders of their recently acquired Polish territory. Songa moved along with the confused masses, unsure of where he was heading. He walked—endless miles—mostly at night. The danger was relentless as the German Luftwaffe kept up a continuous bombing campaign, flying low and destroying everything in its range.

The troops had to share the crowded roads with a massive evacuation of civilian workers and equipment, inching along in the chaos. Whole factories had to be relocated and rebuilt deep in eastern Russia to preserve the industrial production capacity, not the least of which was to make weapons, to give these soldiers some ability to fight back. The road was also choked with panicked refugees, many of whom were reliving a nightmare, forced to flee German invasion for the second time in under two years, having already escaped into the Soviet Union after the Nazi occupation of western Poland in 1939.

The Jewish refugees, in particular, had come to consider the Soviet Union as a somewhat awkward safe haven. When the Nazis orchestrated the non-aggression pact with the Soviet Union, and overtook western Poland in 1939, the Soviets allowed many of the Polish Jews on the border of the demarcation line to cross over to the Soviet side of occupied Poland. The Jewish refugees were absorbed into the Soviet workforce; however, many found themselves on trains to Siberia and other unforgiving locations where they were forced to work for the Communist regime under miserable conditions.

Many others were drafted into the Red Army. Still, they were alive and free from German occupation. The lack of discrimination was well described by one such Polish Jewish refugee in the Soviet Union as "Jews were treated as miserably as everyone else."

The Communist Revolution, and the consequent abolishment of the practice of religion in the Soviet Union, went a long way to suppress the rampant anti-Semitism that existed under the Tsar's rule. Communism, in effect, brought an end to the decades of persecution Jews faced in the Russian empire.

Many Jews in the early days of the movement that led to the Russian Revolution believed that Communism was a powerful vehicle for their equal treatment in Russian society. And to some extent, they were correct. Jews were able to hold high positions in the Soviet system in politics, the military, and in the NKVD: the all-powerful Soviet Secret Police.

Songa, himself, always held himself up as testament to the lack of institutionalized anti-Semitism in the Red Army during the war. He claimed that the fact that he was Jewish never worked against him in his military career, and he eventually rose, along with many other Jews, to high ranks in Stalin's army.

There were roughly one million Jewish soldiers fighting with Allied troops on the Eastern front in World War II, with over 600,000 of those Jewish soldiers serving in the Red Army. Stalin needed bodies, regardless of ethnicity. Their perspective of the Holocaust is unique in that it is not one of a defenseless victim. They, unlike their Jewish civilian counterparts, were spared the dehumanizing horrors of the ghettos, deportations, and concentration camps. Songa was on the front line, facing the gruesomeness of combat, but he was armed. Unlike his family, he was able to fight back.

The hasty retreat of the Red Army left the civilians in the abandoned territories defenseless against the storming German army. The Jews would become the most vulnerable. Melech and Yetta and their family were among those left behind as Nazi prey, poised to face a fate more uncertain and potentially more horrifying than that of their two sons fighting on the front lines.

Within days after the Germans broke the non-aggression pact and invaded the Soviet Union, German paratroopers, who had been dropped and were hiding in the forest near Ozeryany, emerged from the woods and began to occupy the area. Many of the Jewish villagers did not know what to make of the turn of events. Some were relieved to hear of the arrival of the Germans, knowing only that the Soviet occupation would now end.

Melech and Yetta stayed inside, and watched from their windows as the Nazi soldiers marched into Ozeryany. They sat alongside Songa's grandmother, aunts, uncles, and cousins, trying to ascertain the extent of the danger the German occupation posed. It had been only two years earlier when they had endured the *invasion* of the Bolsheviks in their village. This was not unfamiliar. They had learned to survive by watching and waiting. And although a trickle of Polish Jewish refugees had passed through the village, telling tales of unthinkable acts undertaken by the Germans back in their occupied hometowns, the villagers of Ozeryany could only consider these stories to be terrible exaggerations.

Unlike the Soviet occupation, the German occupation brought about perceptible changes almost immediately. The first, most alarming change was with the local Ukrainians. Long the business partners and peaceful co-habitants alongside the Jews, the Ukrainians became increasingly hostile toward their Jewish neighbors. They organized their own police force. Ukrainians began seizing Jewish property: first animals, then equipment, and ultimately land. The Jews had no recourse. While the Jews were stripped of their rights and forced to wear the identifying armband with the blue Star of David, the Ukrainians were clearly enjoying a privileged relationship with their Nazi occupiers.

Long suppressed Ukrainian anti-Semitism was set free, possibly even heightened by the perception that the Soviet occupiers had played

favorites to the Jews during their period of occupation. The arrival of
the Nazi regime was cause for their celebration. Unknown to the Jews
at the time, Hitler had promised to grant the long independence-seek-
ing Ukrainians their own nation, free from Soviet control, in exchange
for their zealous collaboration.

Official "aktions" were decreed. These "aktions" were the German
policies for the Jewish populations in occupied towns. The word would
soon become synonymous with murder, but at this early stage, no one
would understand that. With each successive action, Melech and Yetta
could only believe they had endured the worst and that things could
not deteriorate further.

They watched as Jews were forced into *slave* labor, and ordered to
perform strenuous manual labor—old and young, male and
female—working the fields, digging ditches, and building fortifications
for the Nazi war effort. Often those in forced labor were ordered to
work long days without food or water. Even as they watched Jews literally worked to death, treated as a disposable work force by the Germans, the population held its breath. Nobody in the village could have
imagined the ultimate intent of the German invaders: to make the captured towns *Jew-free*. No one could have conceived that Hitler
intended to annihilate the Jewish population.

◆   ◆   ◆

On the front line of combat, Songa knew nothing of the situation
back home. He was consumed by the daily challenge of staying alive,
against terrible odds, in constant retreat from the seemingly impenetrable German war machine. He continued to move along on foot, his
boots wearing through, leaving his feet exposed. He tied rags around
his bloody feet to protect them, but each step would send a shock of
new pain throughout his body.

The Soviets seemed to have no military strategy. There was no sense
of purpose. The Germans had paralyzed communications networks,

and Songa's infantry unit, stationed on the Western front, never fully knew what they were about to walk into. Artillery and tanks that somehow were not destroyed by German bombers, often stood idle for lack of fuel and transport. If by some miracle there was transport and fuel, then there was no ammunition. Movement of the infantry was often not coordinated, and massive traffic jams would keep them stuck, like sitting ducks. There was nothing but loss—catastrophic loss—and fear.

Everyone was scared, but rumors quickly circulated to the Jewish soldiers to intensify their fear. Getting captured by the Germans could mean certain death if they were identified as Jews. Two weeks into the war, more than a quarter of a million prisoners had been captured. When the Germans took prisoners of war, the security units immediately searched for those who should be killed at once. They weeded out the Jews, often by bribing the Soviet soldiers with additional bread or rations in exchange for singling out their Jewish comrades. There was no time for protest. The *accused* were shot on the spot.

Over five million Soviet soldiers were taken prisoner during the course of the war. Songa's fear of capture was not unfounded. The conditions in the camps were appalling for all POW's, Jew and non-Jew, and the chance of survival became slim for all prisoners, regardless of religion. Fewer than two million of the five million prisoners managed to survive. If the mistreatment by the Nazis did not kill the POWs, Stalin threatened to finish the job: He considered any Red Army soldier taken prisoner to be guilty of treason, and the punishment for falling captive was the same as if one deserted—imprisonment and most likely, death.

Being Jewish offered Songa little additional liability in the Eastern battlefields of World War II. While his family would endure Nazi savagery targeted specifically against Jews, horrifically limiting their chances for survival, Songa faced little discrimination in his odds of dying.

◆   ◆   ◆

Summer slipped into autumn, and autumn heralded the impending alarm that winter would soon be upon them. Survival through another day was Songa's only goal. The early and punishing Soviet winter would bring new misery and challenges in the basic quest to survive. November came, and along with enduring the punishing steps of his cold, bloody feet, Songa had to negotiate the challenge of firing his rifle with the frozen stumps at the end of his hand that were masquerading as fingers.

His uniform was wearing down to threads, the rifles and equipment he and his comrades carried were atrociously outdated, and their faces wore the weary expressions of imminent defeat. He had been in combat for five months, and still, every step backward, every inch of retreat, every acre of territory relinquished to the Fascists, brought Songa new-found despair.

He was hardly alone. The troops were completely demoralized. By December 1941, the Red Army had lost four million men, eight thousand aircraft, and seventeen thousand tanks. Songa had already had his share of narrow escapes from enemy fire. Often he would see the soldier standing next to him reduced to bloody body parts, with just the deafening sound of enemy artillery to warn him that he could very well be next. And he always assumed that he would, in fact, be next.

December brought some good news. Songa listened anxiously as he heard the radio broadcast announcing the Japanese attack on Pearl Harbor. The Americans had been attacked on their own soil. The United States would now surely be entering the war. Only two months earlier, Stalin had appealed to the Americans to open a second front in the war, perhaps in France, to divert some of the German divisions from the Eastern front. He had made it clear to Roosevelt that without this kind of support, along with planes, tanks, and aluminum for production, the Soviet Union would be defeated. His proposals at the time were rejected outright. Now it might be different. The war was now much more than just the Soviet people against the German-Fascist forces.

The night of the radio broadcast, Songa and his comrades cheered and sang and toasted the might of the United States, with many rounds of vodka.

◆   ◆   ◆

It took almost nine months, but his immunity to enemy fire finally ran out. During battle in early 1942, Songa was hit in both legs with shrapnel from mortar fire, wounded, but alert enough to recognize his injuries would not be life threatening. He was taken from the front line to the rear, where some measure of safety could be felt in a makeshift army hospital. For a short time at least, he would have food, shelter, and a warm, dry bed.

It was the first time in nearly a year that Songa slept, really slept, on sheets, without an overly alert subconscious preventing him from being less than ready to fight or run. Songa closed his eyes, and dreamed of his family, his house, and his grandmother's cooking. He relaxed so much that he allowed himself to resurrect his dormant libido, with nurses around him day and night to keep him amused. He loved looking at them, being near them, and being cared for by them. He had forgotten how much pleasure he derived from being around women in his daily life.

One day he could no longer restrain himself, and he made a feeble attempt to proposition one of the nurses. The nurse returned his invitation with a sympathetic stare for the injured soldier. "I am a nun, silly. All the nurses here are nuns." Songa recoiled, clearly disappointed. He closed his eyes and imagined his carefree days in Ozeryany, girls lined up and begging to go out with him.

He recuperated from his injuries and soon was back in the thick of combat. The warm dry sheets and sweet smells of nurses, nuns or not, would once again become a distant memory.

◆   ◆   ◆

The only thing that rivaled the amount of blood flowing from the bodies of Red Army casualties was the amount of vodka flowing through the lips of those soldiers still alive. Food supplies may have been scarce, fuel reserves nearly empty, ammunition virtually depleted, rifles available only for every other soldier (you waited for your comrades to die so you could take their rifle), but the Communist government saw to it that vodka production was adequate, and available in abundant supplies.

The vodka, a ration of one hundred grams before battle, provided anesthesia for the mind. It was what gave Songa and the others the strength and numbed sensibility to climb out of a foxhole upon the commander's signal to attack. It was what allowed Songa to stand, exposed in the open, and charge toward an enemy who was shooting directly at him, armed with a mighty supply of weapons and ammunition. The vodka became a lifeline for Songa, despite the fact that he had never been a drinker prior to the war. But now he was a Russian soldier, and he quickly learned the tricks to make the effects of the alcohol last longer. Drinking animal fat was a favorite—if he was lucky enough to be somewhere with livestock close by—the fat working to line his stomach before he chased down a full glass of vodka. Vodka was one of Songa's few protective shields from his gruesome reality.

Songa's other protective shield was his fantasy of deserting. Desertion was so appealing; he thought of it everyday. "What if I just walked away?" he mused. It was chaos on the battlefield, and it would take days for his commanders to figure out whether he was dead, captured, or simply gone. But Stalin made sure each man understood the consequences of such an act of treason. Stalin, through the NKVD, engaged in the continuous purging of *alleged* defeatists and potential deserters among his front line troops. Red Army troops were under dual command. Every unit was under the control of both a military officer and a military *commissar,* the commissar serving as the watchdog and guardian of what the Soviets referred to as *discipline.*

The commissar had untold power—power to accuse any soldier of suspicious behavior. The NKVD security forces often made arrests, sweeping away to political prisons those considered suspicious. The accused had no rights. Charges were made without evidence. In cases where a strong example was to be set, executions of those charged were carried out on the spot, in front of the soldiers. The message to anyone watching was clear: if you are thinking of deserting or joining the Germans, think again. Ensuring compliance through fear was Stalin's trademark style. Songa learned to keep his mouth shut, and to trust few.

But there was still more to the intersection of war and politics in the Red Army. Stalin was indifferent to the death toll, having thrown millions of soldiers into the line, knowing they would be washed away in defeat. He had no regard for body count. His policies were so unimaginably ruthless that he gave the order that any soldier retreating in the course of battle was to be considered guilty of cowardice and treason. Commanders were told to order their rear line of soldiers to fire upon their comrades should they be *weak* enough to run back in retreat from an overpowering German attack.

There was no regard for the psychological toll inflicted on Soviet soldiers forced to train their guns on their fellow comrades. Red Army soldiers were squeezed between two enemies: the one they faced, and the one within. They lived in constant fear of both the Nazis and the Soviet High Command's unforgiving policies as enforced by the NKVD. Songa understood that no matter whose bullet might take his life, no one would weep for him should he be the next to fall. Death no longer had any meaning.

◆　　　◆　　　◆

By the spring of 1942, both the Germans and the Soviets were working toward a decisive solution to winning the war. Hitler began planning the final destruction of the Soviet army. He had lost his patience for the Red Army's fanatic resistance. He was disgusted with the German army's inability to break the Russian soldiers' will to fight, despite the fact that the Nazis had taken control of so much Soviet territory and had demonstrated clearly superior strength. Hitler set his sights on the South, working to capture the vital grain and oil resources.

Stalin, despite strong intelligence suggesting Hitler's aims, firmly believed the capture of Moscow would continue to be the primary Nazi goal.

By July 20, 1942, Stalin found himself rudely awakened. The Nazis were pounding through lines in the southeast, heading swiftly toward the likely capture of a sprawling industrial city of 500,000 people located on the shores of the Volga River, a city that just happened to have been named for Stalin himself—Stalingrad.

Songa was making his way into Stalingrad, the Don River at his back, with a fast penetrating German army moving toward him. He had just *celebrated* his first anniversary of staying alive in combat, little consolation as the constant hunger, inadequate equipment, and now heightened fear of capture or death plagued every minute of his conscious and subconscious existence.

The Germans managed to pierce Soviet defenses, cross the Don River, and break through directly toward the city of Stalingrad, pounding the city in late August. German bombs were dropped on oil storage tanks that lined the Volga River, on whose banks the city lay, instantly setting fire to the oil storage tanks. The entire area was enveloped in thick plumes of black smoke.

Nazi soldiers captured railway lines and river passages, preventing the flow of food, fuel, and ammunition to the Soviet soldiers and civilians, now caught inside the city of Stalingrad. The Germans savagely bombed the city, residential, and industrial areas alike, destroying any production capabilities and amassing a death toll that led one Red Army soldier to describe the scene of destruction as one where "the ground is slippery with blood."

All around him, Songa could see a city obliterated, reduced to rubble, ash, and carnage. Bodies littered the streets. Dust and ash and smoke permeated the air, making it difficult to breathe. Supplies were nonexistent. Electricity, water supplies, and telephone lines had been destroyed. Songa began to assume, along with all of the other Soviet infantrymen, that he would die in Stalingrad.

Stalin refused to surrender Stalingrad. He would allow no talk of evacuation or withdrawal. "Not a step backward," he declared, asserting the reality that there would soon be no territory left for retreat. The message trickled through to the soldiers on the line.

Songa understood that it was his duty to fight fanatically to the last drop of blood. There was to be a dramatic shift in both the mindset and tactics of the Red Army. Commissar and NKVD control was relaxed, and the military experts were given more oversight. Communist Party rhetoric was replaced with pre-revolution nationalism. National propaganda, to die for Mother Russia, filtered among the troops and throughout the country, along with a planned campaign to inspire frenetic hatred of the German invaders.

Stalin even relaxed the Communist approach of a *classless* army to reinstate special honors, medals, and distinctive uniforms for the officers, as a way to motivate and instill pride. For the first time in years, churches throughout Russia were reopened, and the practice of religion was allowed. This war against the Germans was recast as the Great Patriotic War. Defeat in Stalingrad would signal the defeat of Russia.

Despite the fact that they were severely undermanned and underpowered, the Soviets continued to mount offensive attacks, attempting to grind down the German forces as they themselves absorbed punishing blows and heavy losses.

The civilian population of the city had to be mobilized as reinforcement for the dwindling Red Army, because divisions normally staffed with ten thousand men, were down to one or two hundred men. In Moscow, the Soviet High Command hurriedly planned a major Red Army counter-offensive, the most aggressive and strategic of any initiative since the start of the war. It was determined that at least forty-five days would be necessary to mount the operation. Fresh recruits needed to be trained. The unprecedented production of tanks, artillery, rifles, and ammunition had to be completed. The undetected movement of men and equipment would require time.

In the meantime, the Red Army soldiers trapped in Stalingrad had to accomplish the next to impossible, and hold off defeat. Songa had to fight for survival with nothing more than the refusal to be defeated, a determination that superceded the reality that he was starving, exhausted, tattered, torn, and outnumbered.

German assault troops soon blasted their way into the city. The few remaining Soviet soldiers who survived the assault took shelter wherever they could: in burned-out houses, basements, in the ruins of factories, and other industrial buildings. They watched the exuberant German soldiers move through the streets, drinking and celebrating their imminent victory. Songa, still very much alive, was filled with rage as he watched at close range the faces of his enemy.

The fighting moved to the streets and the ruined buildings, the smoke and fire providing the only screen of daylight cover from the continuous and ruthless German air attack. Battle was different now. Small groups engaged in bloody skirmishes, savagely intimate exchanges, in which Songa would find himself engaged in hand-to-hand combat with the enemy. Lightly armed with dagger and bayonet, Songa would venture from his hiding places, six or seven comrades at his side, moving silently through the ruins, in an attempt to take out unsuspecting German soldiers.

On one such outing, a Nazi soldier thwarted Songa's surprise attack, by spinning around and striking him on the side of the head with the butt of his German rifle. The powerful blow brought Songa to the floor. His vision was bloodied and blurred, but Songa refused to allow that to be the moment of his death. He defiantly grasped his dagger, and through the haze of blood pouring down his face, plunged the dagger squarely into the chest of the enemy soldier. The vision in his wounded eye was badly damaged, but Songa escaped the exchange with his life. He had won the right to continue fighting in the *hell on earth* that was Stalingrad.

Soviet reserves started to trickle into the city to support the battered troops, but in September, after a month of fighting, it was estimated that German forces outnumbered the Soviet forces by more than two-to-one. There was little the Soviets could do other than hang on to what they had: each street, each building, each shop, and each house. The Germans could not be allowed to take control of the city. The Russians had to hold fast until the appointed hour of the planned counter-offensive.

There was no food, and no sleep. But for Songa, even worse than the hunger and fatigue, was the thirst. There was no water. Barges and ferries tried to make their way across the Volga River, loaded with ammunition, light weapons, food rations, water, and anything else they could carry. However, the loss rate was exceptionally high, especially for the bigger boats carrying larger loads.

Both sides began to suffer from the lack of supplies and reinforcements. As mighty as the German Sixth Army might have been at the outset, after two months of Soviet resistance, the German soldiers were wearing down. Exhaustion and fatigue plagued the diminished Nazi army, demoralized by the tactics of street fighting, and their inability to put the Red Army down once and for all and capture the city of Stalingrad. What should have taken two to three days to declare victory was lingering into three months, without a decisive ending.

In mid-October, Hitler made the decision to commit all of the remaining German strength and superiority to finally claim victory in Stalingrad. A massive display of bombing and firepower rained down on the Soviet troops. It was the most ferocious all-out offensive in Stalingrad to date. Hitler was ready to move on with his planned victory over Russia.

Soviet casualties skyrocketed. On October 14, thirty-five hundred wounded men were ferried out of the city, and across the banks of the Volga. This brutal attack should have been the Soviet army's final hour. Miraculously, it wasn't.

Historically, the Russian soldier had an almost mythical image of supernormal strength and stamina, even under the most punishing and adverse conditions. In October 1942, the Red Army soldiers trapped in the inferno that was Stalingrad became part of that mythical legacy. They fended off catastrophe through the sheer will and determination to keep fighting. And now the fanatic resilience of the Soviet defense would tip not just the battle for Stalingrad, but the entire war on the Eastern front, in favor of the Red Army.

The Soviet counter-offensive, named Operation Uranus, was executed on November 19, 1942. The first snow flurries of the winter had arrived three days before. By midnight on the 19th, driving snow was falling, a cold wind drove the temperature down sharply, and more than one million fresh Soviet soldiers were amassed and poised to attack an unsuspecting German army.

The Stalingrad front was on full attack, yet Hitler ignored the advice of his general, and ordered his commander to stay put in Stalingrad rather than abandon the city with what was left of his battle-weary troops. In little more than one week, the Red Army had completely encircled the German's Sixth Army.

By January 1943, the Nazis surrendered. The Red Army soldiers could, most improbably, declare victory over the German forces in Stalingrad. The seemingly invincible Nazi invaders were no longer unstoppable. Now it was the faces of the Nazis, the faces the Soviets had seen only inches away, which were pale, weary, and defeated. The road to ending the war was still long and perilous, but for the first time, Songa and his comrades who managed to survive the carnage of Stalingrad, could believe that there might be a future after all.

4

Facing the Enemy Within

Renewed and recharged from the Stalingrad victory, Songa's loyalty to Stalin and the cause of their Great Patriotic War was stronger than ever. The Red Army moved from a defensive to an offensive mentality. By early spring of 1943, Songa was a lieutenant with increasing responsibility and increasing interest in winning—rather than just surviving—the war. The tide was turning. Songa started to feel more in control, more hopeful.

The shards of optimism were soon shattered. Songa received a letter, his first mail in many, many months. He had heard nothing from his family since the Nazi invasion, almost two years ago. The letter arrived on official stationary, signaling to Songa that the contents would best be left unread. He ripped open the envelope. "I am sorry to inform you of the death of your brother, Josef Ajces," was all Songa could read before he fell to his knees. He forced himself to read on, learning how Josef, embroiled in a fierce tank battle, never made it out of his T-34. He was burned alive by enemy fire. He read the letter again. It was not possible. Josef, his beautiful, fun-loving brother was dead, his body reduced to smoldering ashes. The Germans had killed his brother.

Songa's sense of loss was immeasurable. His mental self-preservation strategy was unraveling. He continually convinced himself that if he could stay alive during this war, so too could every member of his family. He didn't allow himself to imagine further about his other family members. Instead, he refreshed his already fervent patriotic desire for victory, with the taste of revenge for his brother's death. He would kill every German within his reach. The Germans would have to drain him of every last drop of blood before he would give up the fight.

He was soon thwarted in his quest for vengeance, and the obstacle came not from the Germans, but from the Soviets. It would be the invisible and insidious *enemy within* that would inflict the war's most toxic blows against Songa. All he wanted to do was kill German soldiers, but the Red Army—the institution he so admired, and to which he had given his profound loyalty—would take him away from the front line. He would not be able to accomplish his goal. Songa was poised to face the untold indignities and nightmarish consequences of a totalitarian government and military. He was about to experience the tactics of a regime that boosted itself through paranoid suspicion, the presumption of guilt, and a strategy of ensuring unquestioning compliance through terror and torture.

At the outset of the invasion of the Soviet Union, Stalin commanded that all Red Army units should be "purged of unreliable elements," and that any officers and men coming out of German encirclements alive should be thoroughly investigated by the NKVD to root out the "German spies" among them. "Death to the spies," was a favorite post-battle cry sounded by the commissars, the strong-armed disciplinarians of the Red Army, looking to place blame for defeat.

It was a no win situation for the combat-battered officers and troops. Surviving a battle where the Nazis claimed victory, and avoiding capture by the enemy only led them to the path of suspicion and possible condemnation by the NKVD. A *Special Sections* unit of the NKVD collected detailed information on the morale and battle performance of individual soldiers and officers within units. Such was the latitude and breadth of the NKVD's power to accuse that among the charges that could bring a sentence of imprisonment or death to soldiers was panic-mongering, drunkenness, incompetence, and abandoning battle-stations (which could merely equate to getting lost).

Songa had only recently been made a lieutenant when the Germans overran a position his unit was holding. His unit suffered a large number of casualties, although he himself came away unharmed. Songa knew the defeat could carry dangerous repercussions with the NKVD. He had heard the rumors of men disappearing, or even shot based on accusations of treachery. It was impossible to be a Red Army soldier and not be aware of the fear and terror tactics of the NKVD. But in the days following his defeat, he heard nothing.

It happened several months later. Several NKVD officials approached him at the Front and abruptly ordered him to come with them. Bewildered, but unquestionably compliant, Songa silently followed their orders. Songa's mind raced with possible explanations for what was happening to him, but with little information from his captors, he was left to imagine the worst. His instincts told him to say nothing.

The NKVD officials escorted him to the closest train station. Flanked by the officials, he was forced to board the next train, and began a wordless journey. He didn't dare ask where they were going.

After traveling for many excruciating hours, and hundreds of miles, he finally understood his destination.

They were en route to the remote region of Uzbekistan in Soviet Central Asia. As he had feared, the NKVD was taking him to a political prison, near Tashkent. He was being charged with espionage. The NKVD officials went so far as to allege that they had pictures of Songa talking to an SS officer in Berlin. The punishment for such treason was death.

As of 1943, Songa had never set foot in Berlin. He had never colluded with the Nazis. He hated the Germans with all of the patriotic fervor of the time, and he was fiercely loyal to the Red Army, to the war effort, and even to Stalin himself. He was a survivor of the battle of Stalingrad; he should have been recognized for his heroism rather than vilified as a traitor.

But there was no room for the truth in the tyrannical reign of the NKVD. Songa stood accused. In a mockery of judicial process, with no reasonable chance for defense, the NKVD simply expected him to confess to his crimes.

Songa had already lived through gruesome battle, but the intent to harm in battle is dispensed generically. The punishment was intended for anyone and everyone who stood behind the opposing front line. Now he had been singled out, and the torture was personal, individually directed at him, to slowly and methodically unravel his very being.

Enemy fire can mercifully kill, instantly. Psychological manipulation and physical deprivation inflicts relentless, insidious, lingering suffering. The tactics used by the NKVD would demonstrate evil beyond anything the already desensitized young officer could ever imagine.

After days of travel, Songa arrived at the prison complex near Tashkent. No one spoke to him. Upon arrival he was thrown into a cell with other alleged political prisoners. It was a cramped, dank, concrete room, with nothing to fill it but accused men and the horrific stench emanating from their crowded, unwashed bodies, and the human waste they produced. There was no place to sit, and no one dared to sit on the floor. Standing upright was considered too comfortable for the prisoners, and Songa was directed to assume a crouching position—knees bent, hands in the air—for hours on end. Should his hands go down, Songa was beaten. Should he fall to the floor from exhaustion, he was beaten.

The formal interrogations began: relentless, mind numbing interrogations. Songa would sit, hour-after-hour, bombarded with lies and false accusations. "Admit to your crimes, Comrade," he was admonished. Of course no purported photographs documenting his alleged collusion with the Nazis were ever produced.

Days slipped into nights, and soon Songa began to lose track of time. He was not permitted to sleep. Traitors did not deserve the luxury of sleep. Every time he fell asleep, the NKVD officials would wake him and take him in for interrogation, demanding that he confess to his crime. Sleep deprivation was a favorite form of torture for the

NKVD, and a particularly effective means for getting prisoners to *crack* during interrogation.

Day-after-day, the pattern repeated itself, and day-after-day, Songa would not, or more accurately, could not, admit to treason. Songa hated the Nazis. The Nazis had killed his brother. The Nazis had killed his comrades. The Nazis were committing unknown atrocities against his family and friends, and his homeland. He could not admit to aiding their murderous efforts. The NKVD insisted that he sign the paperwork—the declaration that he was a spy. But Songa would not sign.

The longer he was imprisoned, the more he trusted his initial instincts about the NKVD's strategy for forced confession. Songa surmised that they would not kill him if he did not sign the paperwork. Whatever happened, he determined that signing meant death.

He had to endure the daily prison *death march*, where he was rounded up, marched out into the courtyard, and told to put his hands against the wall. As the guard raised his rifle in Songa's direction, Songa never knew whether that would be the day the trigger would be pulled. He would not confess.

The NKVD repeatedly threatened to execute him for *not* signing the confession, but he stuck with his strategy, and refused to yield. "I'll be punished, but I'll be alive," he repeatedly told himself. "I won't sign."

Time crept by. With no sleep, and no food, Songa existed on a meager ration of black bread and watery soup, just enough to keep him from dying of starvation. He began to waste away both physically and mentally. His ability to withstand the beatings and the psychological torture, even for this man of supernormal strength and determination, was starting to erode.

He had no idea how much time had elapsed since he was taken prisoner, but he judged that months of his life must have vanished, based on his deteriorated physical appearance. He had lost an unimaginable amount of weight, all of his teeth were loose, and his unshaven face now produced a beard that grew down past his neck toward his collarbone. He should have been dead by now, but he was still alive, which was, in itself, part of the torture.

He finally reached his breaking point. One night, in a semi-delusional state, Songa decided that even death would be a welcome relief to this punishing existence. He would confess to the espionage charges at the next interrogation. He would tell his accusers anything they wanted to hear. He would betray himself so that he could end the suffering. He would sign the paperwork.

That day, the day the Communists *broke* Songa—the day he decided that even death would be preferable to continuing to breathe in this nightmarish existence—turned out to be the day Songa *broke* the NKVD. Officials intercepted his planned confession with the news that they were done with him, and that he would be released from the political prison.

Emotionally and physically shattered though he was, even in his delusional state, Songa could absorb the knowledge that his strategy was successful, and that he had withstood the NKVD. He had survived the brainwashing, the interrogation, the starvation, and the humiliation. He had accomplished what most men could not. He had impressed the NKVD with his stamina and resilience, forcing them to draw the conclusion that he was more of an asset to them alive, than dead.

NKVD officials arranged for Songa's release from the political prison, but rather than simply releasing him, they decided to transfer him to a *normal* prison, not far from the political prison, one that housed ordinary, genuine criminals. It was here, among the usual crew of murderers and thieves that Songa felt like a free man. Here, in this prison, as he sat among felons, he endured no more interrogations. His food rations were significantly more generous. He was allowed to sleep. He knew when it was night, and when it was day. There were no more daily courtyard marches to the wall. He no longer had a death sentence hanging over his head.

Almost a year passed in confinement. Millions of people continued to die as the war waged on, and 1943 slipped into 1944. Songa had little idea of what was happening back on the frontlines, or in the outside world. And then, one morning, no different from any other morning since his confinement, and consistent with the whole surreal experience, a guard came into Songa's cell, and simply said, "You can go."

◆   ◆   ◆

Just as abrupt as his dismissal from the front lines, was his reentry into the outside world. He was expected to resurface in the war-ravaged world, to simply pick up where he had left off. He was given nothing when he was told to leave the prison—no instructions where to go, or what to do. He walked out the prison gates, free, only in a most illusory notion of freedom.

Songa left prison with only the clothes on his back: the tattered uniform he had arrived in all those months ago, now a young man of twenty-eight, who looked sixty. He had nothing. He knew nothing of his family. He knew nothing of the location of his unit, or the progress of the war. His loyalty to the Red Army had been betrayed by unthinkable torture. It was winter, and he knew only that he was somewhere in Uzbekistan.

He walked aimlessly, mile after mile, towering piles of snow flanking him on both sides of the road. He followed the road through the outskirts of the city of Tashkent. Walking through this region of Soviet Central Asia, populated by Tadzhiks, Songa felt as though he had entered another country. The natives of this region were culturally and ethnically very different from the Russians. They hated Communism and they hated Stalin. As best as they could, they tried to retain their own traditions.

Songa was freezing, and he knew he could not last much longer. "Maybe they won after all," he thought to himself, thinking of the NKVD. "Maybe this is my death march."

Suddenly, in the distance, against the bleak winter landscape, he saw a local Tadzhik man working, just a few steps off the road. Songa struggled to move toward the man, stopping a few feet away. The Tadzhik watched his approach, eyeing Songa cautiously, mistrustful of this strangely aged young officer in his Red Army uniform. Songa stood without speaking, careful to keep his distance.

The Tadzhik was in the process of constructing a house, which was more of a glorified hut by Songa's standards. Typically, Tadzhik homes were primitive: the entire house consisted of one large room with a clay roof, a big pit dug into the middle of the floor for lighting fires.

After a time, Songa moved a few steps closer to the man and addressed him in Russian. "Can I help you?" Songa asked, in a tone that was more of a plea than an offer of assistance. "I can work for you in exchange for some bread and shelter."

The man stared at Songa's uniform. He was no lover of Communism, or Stalin, and was wary of Songa's motives. But the picture he saw when he looked at Songa's face, the picture of a young man—emaciated and grotesquely damaged by incarceration and war—dispelled any mistrust of Songa's motives. Looking beyond the exterior, the Tadzhik was able to see a decent man who was hungry, cold, and willing to work in exchange for food.

"You have a deal," the Tadzhik told him. "Now let's get you inside before you freeze to death." They walked a few yards past the construction site to the house where the Tadzhik currently lived with his wife and daughter. After a few days, Songa had proven himself to be a useful and honest worker. Over time, he told the family his story—where he had grown up, his experiences in the war, and the details of his imprisonment. Songa's natural charms took hold, and he was embraced as a member of the family. For Songa, far removed from the front lines of battle, and anything familiar from his past life, this unexpected interlude proved to be a very nourishing time of emotional and physical healing.

It had been years now since Songa had been with his own family. Spending time with this surrogate family connected him with his past, with a time that seemed so distant. Could it be that there was once a time when life was happy and peaceful? Songa thought to himself, in bemused wonder, about the life he once led, where he had the luxury of worrying about mundane things. For the past two years, his thoughts were consumed with nothing more than trying to stay alive.

Several weeks passed, and Songa knew that his brief reprieve from the horrors of war and Soviet totalitarianism would have to end. Living a life that was something other than a daily struggle for survival was simply not an option as long as the Nazis stood on Soviet soil. As the war raged on, every able-bodied Soviet man was expected to be part of the war effort. After his release from prison, Songa was not actively engaged in the war effort. He had no deliberate intentions to shirk his military duties. When he left prison, he had been given no instructions or orders. Eventually, Soviet authorities caught up with him, and labeled him a deserter. He was arrested, again.

This time Songa was not sent to prison. He was required to report for service in the Soviet equivalent of a suicide squad—the so-called "Punishment Battalion." The Punishment Battalion was one of the mechanisms the Red Army used to wear down German forces. The troops consisted of men believed to be guilty of a crime against the Soviet Union; they were viewed as cannon fodder for German ammunition. The soldiers in these battalions were sent to participate in the most difficult and dangerous battles against the Germans. The odds of survival for the missions of the Punishment Battalion were virtually zero. The Red Army was a ruthlessly unforgiving institution, and Songa was forced, once again, to confront that ruthlessness head on.

In the cacophony that had become his life, embroiled in the dehumanizing politics of Stalinism, this time Songa found a perverse comfort in his arrest. Placement in the Punishment Battalion meant he was fighting again, and the hatred and desire to defeat the Nazis was rekindled within him. The punitive circumstances, and slim chances for survival were mentally oppressive, but the fact remained that Songa was a soldier.

On a visceral level, he was recharged. Given the alternative he had experienced in political prison, it was far more preferable to die in the course of battle, at the hand of a hated and obvious enemy, than to die from starvation and torture by your fellow citizens. And while hope for survival was slim, word spread through the punishment battalion that anyone who managed to remain alive after three months of service would be considered *rehabilitated*, and would be allowed to return to regular service.

He had been through Stalingrad. He had survived political prison. And so, Songa, as he had done throughout the war, defied the terrible odds against him. He managed to dodge enemy fire for the full three months of service in the Punishment Battalion.

As promised, his survival allowed him the right to return to his regular service, with all of the privileges of a Soviet officer restored. After almost fifteen months, Songa returned to his unit and resumed his former command position as a Lieutenant.

When he returned, his fellow soldiers looked at him as though they were looking at a ghost. No one expected him to survive after his disappearance. But he was back with his comrades, his brothers-in-arms. He looked around, taking inventory of the many missing faces. The casualties had continued to mount in his absence, and yet, here he was, still among the living. Songa felt strong. He once again felt that he had some control. The knowledge that someone close to him might have been the one to betray him made him even stronger: he was now even more vigilant and conscious of the need for self-preservation.

Shortly after his return, Songa received papers issued by the authority of the High Command, officially clearing him of all of the charges against him. He was once again considered trustworthy, and he resumed what would become a very promising and successful military career.

Ironically, surviving the incarceration, the torture, the Punishment Battalion, and all of the other unspeakable acts against him in the name of suspected treason, may have served to boost his military career prospects and his standing. His inexplicable knack for surviving worked in his favor as well. Each time the more senior officers were killed, they had to be immediately replaced by underlings who remained standing. Songa was gaining more and more authority, often simply because he was the last man standing.

5

The Tide Turns

By the time Songa returned to his command at the front, it was the spring of 1944, and was a completely different war from the one he had left all those months ago. The Red Army was buoyed by its victories, as well as America's full participation as an ally in the war. The formerly ill-equipped troops now had a surplus of weapons and supplies, and consisted of revitalized, organized, well-trained, and adequately outfitted soldiers whose morale was strong. They believed they would win the war.

Life for Songa in this Red Army had improved significantly as compared to the hellish existence he had experienced during the first three years of war. With the American supplies flowing in, officers could basically get whatever they needed. He had plenty of food. He had vodka. And he had cigarettes, the prize of all prizes. As an officer, he enjoyed significant comforts not enjoyed by the lower ranks. While the enlisted men often slept on the cold, hard ground, or more likely, in the mud, officers were pampered with makeshift quarters that even had beds in which they could sleep.

In June of 1944, the American forces had landed in France, opening the long sought-after second front against the Germans. This news allowed Stalin to become more and more confident about the ultimate outcome of the war. He began to plan his vision for the post-war New World Order, one that would ensure the expansion of Communism and ensure his personal power across the borders of the Soviet Union's neighboring countries.

One of Stalin's key political desires was the undoing of the borders drawn by the Treaty of Versailles at the end of World War I, which gave Poland independence from the former Russian empire. In the early days of World War II, as a result of the non-aggression pact between Hitler and Stalin, Poland was occupied within days. The Germans marched into western Poland, while the Soviets occupied eastern Poland. In the confusion and chaos, the Polish government fled to London. What remained of the defeated Polish army, under the leadership of General Sikorski (and later General Anders), went into exile as well.

Eventually, Hitler attacked the Soviet Union. The Soviet Union was then thrust into an unexpected alliance with the British, and the Soviets, historically bitter enemies to the Poles, suddenly found themselves on the same side of the war as the Poles. Red Army soldiers, who had brutally crushed the Polish Army in 1939, now fought the Germans alongside those same Polish soldiers they once tried to kill and capture.

Stalin's goal was to capitalize on the Soviet Union's role as the liberator of occupied Poland, and create a new, strong Polish Communist Party under the name "The Polish Workers' Party," (PPR, from the Polish translation). His intention was to gain favor with the mainstream Poles, and to have his Communist Polish Workers' Party emerge as the ruling political party in post-war Poland.

The *PPR* as it was called, tried to appeal to Poland's citizens during the war. Thinly disguised as patriots fighting for Polish independence, the party members represented themselves as having goals similar to those of the exiled Polish government in London. With the nationalistic Polish Home Army still operating, a major initiative of Stalin's Polish Communist party was to create a new Polish army, in effect *competing* with the existing exiled Polish Army.

In Stalin's mind, this new Polish army would be populated by the vast numbers of Polish refugees, many of who were Jews, who had escaped into the Soviet Union after the Germans invaded Poland. This newly formed, Communist controlled Polish Army, the LWP, or Polish People's Army, would be entirely under the direction of Stalin. Engineered as a satellite of the Red Army, the Polish People's Army would fight the Germans in Poland and plant the seeds for a smooth Communist takeover of post-war Poland.

The Soviet-controlled Polish Army needed leaders with experience. Since Polish officers were scarce, and more importantly, not trusted, Stalin commissioned many Red Army officers to move into leadership positions in the new Polish Army. Jews were particularly desirable, since there was little fear of Jewish soldiers deserting to join the Germans. Songa, a Jewish junior Red Army officer, reared within the Polish borders and educated in Polish, was an optimal choice for such an assignment.

In 1944, Songa was transferred from the Red Army to the new Polish Army. He unwittingly assumed a highly political role: he not only was to fight a war, but also, in the process, was to forge popular Polish support for the Communist army, one that would become a decisive force in post-war Poland. He was commissioned as a lieutenant in the First Polish Army, 4th Division of Infantry, under the command of Jan Kilinski. He was given a Polish Army uniform, and began a new chapter in his military career.

For Songa, the politics at the time were unimportant. He still did not consider himself a Communist. He continued to make it clear that he hated the ideology of Communism. But he was wiser now, and had, unfortunately, learned from his experiences. He knew how the game was played, how to suppress his true sentiments, and how to go along with the party rules. "Assimilation is survival," his father's words echoed.

Songa was, at the core, a soldier engaged in a war, driven by his intense desire to defeat the Germans, restore order, and return to his family. His goals were clear. Whether he achieved them in a Red Army uniform or a Polish Army uniform did not make much of a difference to him. He didn't think beyond the end of the war. He understood that his ability to assimilate into the environment as required would serve him well, even potentially presenting some fresh opportunities in the newly formed army.

◆   ◆   ◆

By the early summer of 1944, Songa and his men exuberantly pushed across the Soviet Union border into Poland. Each day saw the liberation of a new town, village, or city. Several months earlier, Songa's own home village of Ozeryany and the entire Ukraine fell into Soviet hands once again. Knowing that the Germans were on the run filled the Soviet soldiers with a sense of newfound invincibility after all of the years of fighting. However, as Songa and his troops moved through and liberated the formerly occupied regions, his exuberance was drastically tempered by his firsthand observation of the extent of the German devastation and destruction to his homeland and its people.

What Songa saw could never be adequately described. Entire towns were reduced to rubble, nothing more than burnt-out remnants of once vital and flourishing communities. As he moved through these towns, village survivors told him stories detailing Nazi atrocities of such unimaginable proportion—of crimes so heinous—that even men like Songa, who had endured four long years of battle, could not wholly accept these stories as truth.

Stories circulated of the slaughter of entire populations of villages. If the Germans suspected that someone in the town had been sympathetic to local partisans, the whole population would be locked in a barn and the barn set on fire, leaving all the villagers, Jew and non-Jew, to burn to death. There were accounts of Nazi soldiers snatching babies from their mothers, drowning the babies in barrels of water as the mothers were forced to watch. Many survivors gave reports of mass executions of men, women, and children by the Einsatzgruppen—the mobile killing squads of the SS, whose job, it was later discovered, was to murder every Jew, gypsy, and political dissident in captured towns.

Slowly, Songa began to believe and to understand the extent of the Nazi barbarism. There was too much consistency in the stories he heard. And the more Songa saw, the more he was transformed, understanding that there were no rules in this war. He began to take justice into his own hands, and adopted a firm *take no prisoners* ethos.

At the conclusion of a battle, Songa would send his men to round up any surviving German soldiers. With the same subtle gesture each time, he conveyed the order that none of these prisoners should return alive. Once their intelligence potential had been determined and exploited, soldiers captured under his command always met with a *mishap*. Songa had no use for German prisoners of war. In his mind, he was a witness to their villainy, and needed no further convincing of their guilt. He believed they did not deserve so much as the crumbs of bread that would be necessary to keep them alive.

As punitive as Songa felt toward the Germans, it wasn't until a day in June 1944, that he saw what would become his ultimate justification for ensuring that no Nazi was ever given the privilege of living, as long as he personally had some control over the situation. On that fateful day, he finally understood the unthinkable evil the Germans had carried out against his own brethren—the attempted extermination of European Jewry.

◆　　　◆　　　◆

Songa was moving with his troops toward the outskirts of Lublin, Poland when they happened upon some sort of complex in the nearby town of Majdanek. It looked like it had been recently abandoned. Unsure of what they had found, the Soviet troops investigated, walking past an area framed by a main gate. Two guard posts sat perched on either side of the gate. The entire complex was surrounded by barbed wire. Songa's unit stood alongside several Red Army divisions as they moved cautiously into the camp. They were about to uncover the world's first encounter with the evidence and inner workings of one of Hitler's systematic killing centers.

As the soldiers wandered into the camp, they tried to make sense of what lay before them. Nothing in the modern human experience could prepare them for what they were seeing. Some, even after four years of absorbing the sights and smells of war and blood and body parts, now simply froze in their tracks and wept, unable to take another step forward. Songa forced himself to move through slowly, but stoically, as he tried to process the sight before his eyes.

He saw emaciated bodies, some standing, some laying on the ground, clothed in worn striped camp uniforms, alive, but almost skeletal figures that were indiscernible as male or female. He moved on with a group of soldiers to an area behind what looked like makeshift sleeping barracks. As they turned, they were assaulted with the hellish sight of a pile of human bodies and skeletons, a ghastly mound seemingly waiting for some kind of burial. Behind the mound they discovered the intended destination of those human remains: Majdanek's crematorium and gas chambers. The smell of burnt human flesh and hair permeated the air with such ferocity that many of the liberating soldiers vomited violently and had trouble breathing. Songa kept his composure. This sickening smell, they would later learn, was the result of the daily burning of corpses in the overworked ovens housed in the crematorium: An estimated 350,000 people had been gassed and burned in the Majdanek concentration camp in the very spot where Songa now stood.

Songa continued walking. He moved, not through any conscious effort of his own, but through the gravitational pull of a man realizing that with each step he was descending further and further into an inferno. He entered another building and came face to face with the ghosts of Majdanek's dead, by way of their shoes. The Nazis had established a shoe repair station at Majdanek where the confiscated prisoner shoes were reconditioned and ultimately sent to German civilians. Songa now stood in a room, surrounded by tens of thousands of shoes, piled in mounds that reached to the ceiling. The shoes told the stories of the victims who had passed through those gates—old worn shoes, shoes of the wealthy, shoes of men, women, and most horrifically, mounds and mounds of shoes that once rested on the feet of laughing babies and children.

He rejoined several other soldiers, saying nothing. Time had frozen. They did not know how long they had been in the camp. Suddenly they were awakened from their daze when they realized a few of the prisoners were moving toward them. The prisoners were staring at the soldiers through their sunken eye sockets, looks of disbelief carved out of their wasted faces. Songa wondered how these prisoners had managed to stay alive in this place that would redefine humanity's definition of evil. He quickly realized that among the death and destruction, he had to focus on the living. These people would be the only source of explanation for what had happened inside those barbed wires.

"Don't feed anyone," the order was quickly passed. Not to offer some of their meager army rations to these starving skeletons took great restraint. But Songa understood that to feed such grotesquely malnourished people could possibly kill them. How perverse it would be to survive the Nazis, only to die by the helping hands of the liberators. But still, not everyone followed the orders, and Songa saw several soldiers handing out food rations to the prisoners. He turned his back and walked away, not wanting to watch the potential outcome.

As Songa turned, a man in a striped uniform shuffled toward him, just close enough to be heard. He opened his mouth, and in a barely audible voice croaked out the words "are you here to save us?" Songa choked back his tears, and answered in Polish, reassuring the prisoner. "They are all gone," the prisoner whispered to Songa. Songa did not understand what the man meant. "Who?" he started to respond, but before he could get the word out, he felt his chest tighten. The landscape blackened and he felt a chill, despite the warm air temperature. Songa realized that this shell of a human being was speaking to him, not in Polish, but in Yiddish. The bodies, the human remains, the shoes—everything he had seen—it suddenly became clear. These were Jews who had died here.

Until that June day in 1944, Songa hated the Nazis with the patriotic fervor of a soldier defending his homeland against a vicious and rapacious enemy. He knew what the Germans had done to the towns and villages they had occupied. He knew that in the heat of battle, the Nazis killed his brother, Josef. But the Majdanek experience brought his hatred to such a new depth, to a level of sadness and anguish that could never be extinguished simply by military victory. His discovery of the mass extermination of so many people who were just like him, made the whole war experience intensely personal. The optimism and sense of hope that had been evolving, as the Allied victory became more apparent, was shattered. Songa knew that, no matter who ultimately won the war, he, as a Jew, could never feel anything other than defeated.

6

Where is Home

With the continued liberation of occupied towns and cities, and the continued discovery through eyewitness and survivor accounts of the Nazi atrocities, Songa knew he had to find a way to return home to Ozeryany and find his own family. As the Polish and Soviet armies continued the westward advance against the rapidly fleeing Germans, many soldiers had the opportunity to return to their hometowns. Some were lucky enough to be the proud liberators, and others marched into the post-liberation chaos to search for loved ones. Songa was eager to act on his own dreams of returning to a liberated Ozeryany. In the fall of 1944, he finally had the opportunity.

He was given forty-eight hours and a horse. He rode as quickly as he could, not stopping to eat or sleep. After almost a full day of travel, he came to the area surrounding Ozeryany. Songa slowed his frenetic pace as he surveyed all that used to be vibrant and thriving. The normally controlled and rigidly disciplined officer was unprepared to accept the fact that the same devastation he had witnessed across the Soviet landscape had also afflicted his own home region.

The Germans were gone on that day, but their legacy was alive in what remained, or more accurately, what did not remain. The beautiful woods, lakes, abundant fruit orchards, smells, and sounds of nature that had enveloped him as a child were gone. The land, which should have been a blaze of early fall color and wildlife, instead bore the remnants of the Nazi *scorched earth* policy, where, in retreat, the Germans burned and destroyed everything they left behind.

As he moved closer to the town, the shattering image that confronted him proved almost too much to absorb. Songa came to a virtual standstill as he looked around. He saw a devastated and defiled land. The village that once provided sustenance, shelter, and community to everyone he loved, and who had loved him, was gone.

Perched high on his horse and crisply dressed in his army uniform, his appearance was grotesquely incongruous with the view before him. He scanned the area as a mounting feeling of despair started to replace the hopefulness, and he looked anxiously for something familiar of the town he left five long years ago. The fantasy that had sustained him all those years, the image of heroically liberating his parents, grandmother, aunts, and uncles, the image of his father embracing him and finally acknowledging all that he had accomplished, was slipping away from him.

After some brief minutes of increasingly frantic searching, Songa eventually was able to reorient himself to find his street. He dismounted and led his horse slowly through the ash and rubble, down the barely recognizable street, toward home. He looked at the fragments of what had been his neighbors' homes, and then stopped abruptly as he caught a glimpse of what he did not want to see. What should have been his house, once grand and sturdy, the only house in the village made of brick and fieldstone, the house that had always been filled with music and love and family, was now nothing more than a foundation and a few fragments of exterior walls.

When Songa came upon his house, and saw nothing more than the remnants of his home—stripped of life, stripped of the possessions that filled the house and identified his family and its traditions, even stripped of its exterior walls that had formed the safe, insulating perimeter around his large, loving family—his mind and heart raced with unthinkable thoughts.

He had to find his parents. As he moved through the town, an intimidating figure in full military regalia, walking among the downtrodden and cautious Ukrainians, he began to fire questions at those milling about. As enthusiastic collaborators with the Nazis, many of the Ukrainians wore their guilt on their faces. They were terrified of this Soviet officer who was becoming increasingly impatient. Slowly Songa began to notice that of the few people walking in what was left of the streets of Ozeryany, none were Jewish.

After several interactions, someone told Songa to speak to a man at the train station. This man would know something about his family and could help to answer his questions. Becoming mad with anxiety and desperation, Songa found the man at the train station, a local Ukrainian. Rational behavior was disappearing now from the normally self-disciplined officer. Acting completely on impulse and adrenaline, Songa reached for his weapon, approached the unsuspecting man, and pressed his gun against the man's temple. "Tell me where my parents are or I will blow your brains out," he hissed. The Ukrainian didn't stop to doubt the sincerity of the threat, and fearing for his life at the hands of this seemingly unhinged army officer, nervously told him what he knew. "They are gone," the man told him. "They are not here." Songa listened intently to the entire story as his armed hand shook with mounting rage.

When the Nazis came into Ozeryany in 1941, they followed their standard plan for occupation. In the beginning, people stayed in their homes as the German government moved into town. All of the Jews were ordered to identify themselves by wearing a round yellow patch on the front and back of their clothes. The girls, in particular, were terrified to leave the house, as the German soldiers were known to make sexual slaves out of them, taking them for days at a time, raping them and beating them until they were barely conscious. Homes were looted, and the Jews were required to hand over all valuable items—gold, fur, and jewelry, whatever they had. Ukrainians began to seize Jewish land and property, shamelessly turning their backs on previous decades of camaraderie with their Jewish neighbors.

As time went on, the Nazis created a ghetto for the Jews, consolidating them with the Jews from the neighboring village of Warkowicze, crowding them all into a few square blocks, and isolating them from the rest of the town. In the villages with sparse populations, ghetto conditions were not as horrific as those in the larger cities, however, city or village, the people were starving. For a while the ghetto remained open. With appropriate permission, one could come and go to perform work duty. The work permit was seen as a ticket for survival, as the Jews reasoned that as long as they could serve a useful purpose to the Germans—as slave labor—they would remain safe.

On October 4, 1942, the order was given to seal the ghetto. From that day on no one could leave. By that time, the rumors were well circulated to indicate that the sealing of the ghetto was synonymous with liquidation. Many Jews continued to believe the Nazi lies and propaganda promising that all ghetto residents were to be relocated to a work camp. But many other Jews were tipped off that being caught in the ghetto after it was sealed would mean certain death. They took to the woods and enacted plans to go into hiding. An extremely sympathetic and courageous neighboring Czech farming community took many of the escapees into hiding. A number of Ozeryany's Jews, therefore, were able to escape the ghetto before it was sealed.

Once the ghetto was sealed, those who were trapped inside had no chance of escaping. One morning, the remaining Jews were rounded up, separated by gender, and marched out of the ghetto. Groups of men and women were then instructed to walk out of the town to a nearby forest, two kilometers from the village. The Ukrainian police willingly, and in some cases enthusiastically, assisted with this roundup and transport. In the forest stood a bridge, and on either side of the bridge were freshly dug ditches.

The Jews of Ozeryany and other neighboring villages—Songa's family, friends, teachers, and everyone who played a role in his life as a child and a young man—were ordered to strip naked, leave their clothing and belongings in a mounting pile, and line up, in batches, on the bridge. One-by-one, Nazi soldiers approached the Jews, put a pistol to their heads, and squeezed the trigger. Only one bullet per person was allowed. Dead or alive, each person dropped into the ditch. Young Jewish boys were ordered to organize the layer of fallen bodies to make room for the next batch.

Witnesses contend that Songa's mother, Yetta, grandmother, Miriam, and his Aunt Ziesel, met with this horrific fate. They were rounded up together with other women and taken to the nearby area of Mizoc, where they were executed. Songa's Uncle Avrum was also spotted in a similar transport, and presumably was murdered in a similar manner. Songa's sister, Rose, had been in an institution for the mentally impaired when the Germans marched into the area, and had been executed almost immediately after the Nazi occupation.

The details of Songa's father's death were not as clear; it was certain, however, that zealously collaborating Ukrainians killed Melech Ajces, rather than the Nazis. Two conflicting accounts circulated of his father's tragic end. One witness claimed to have seen Melech rounded up with several other Jewish men, and brought to a wooden barn. There, Ukrainian peasants locked the door and set the barn on fire, leaving those inside to slowly burn to death while the peasants stood by and watched. Another witness claimed to have seen Melech shot point blank by the Ukrainian police.

When the Ukrainian man at the train station finished talking, Songa, whose hands by this time were shaking uncontrollably, withdrew his gun from the man's head and walked away. Then he snapped. His four years of emotional stoicism and control, his four years of absorbing the sights, sounds, smells, and fear of war, now erupted. His parents, and virtually all of his immediate family were dead, brutally murdered.

He had deluded himself into believing that his beautiful, benevolent, gentle, caring family would be saved, would be immune from the savagery of the Nazis and the Ukrainians. Once that delusion was shattered, he was undone. Songa went literally crazy during those next hours that followed his discovery of the truth. He ranted and raved and cried out his anguish in the streets of Ozeryany. He shot his pistol into the air, aiming at no one, and everyone, simultaneously. Until the day he died, the scars of the total and utter devastation he felt during those hours were never healed. He had saved so many, but of the people he loved most, he had saved no one.

◆   ◆   ◆

Out of the entire Feinblatt/Ajces family of eight aunts and uncles, as well as siblings and cousins, only one immediate family member had survived the Nazi occupation of Ozeryany: Songa's Aunt Ruchel, the youngest of Yetta's siblings. Ruchel was married, with a two-year-old daughter, Malka, at the time of Nazi occupation. Her husband, Herschel, had been among the Jews able to work outside the ghetto, securing a job in a flourmill just outside Ozeryany. Herschel was tied into the information network and understood that the day would come that the Nazis would exterminate all of the Jews of Ozeryany. He had planned for a hiding place for his family when it would become necessary to *disappear*.

He had approached several neighboring Czech farmers to enquire about their willingness to hide his family. Herschel had been in the fruit wholesale business prior to the Soviet occupation, and had good relationships with many of these farmers. However, no one wanted to take the risk. Finally, a poor and often drunk farmer offered to hide them, knowing that Herschel's family had money and that their survival could be lucrative for him. Arrangements were made and money exchanged hands.

One day, word came of the Ukrainian police gathering up a group of Ukrainian men, and taking them to the forest to dig ditches. The Jews who heard this story understood that these ditches were to be their future mass graves. They had heard the stories often enough from those who had run away from countless other occupied towns to the west. Ozeryany was actually one of the last towns to be liquidated. The actions were taken almost a year after other Polish towns to the west had suffered similar fates. It was September 1942, and Herschel knew it was time for him, and his family, to disappear.

A six-foot by six-foot hole had been dug under the stable in the cooperating farmer's barn. That hole, or *room*, as they euphemistically called it, would become Ruchel, Herschel, and Malka's home. The grownups could not stand in the hole, so they sat, or crouched in the dark space for twenty-two hours a day. The only light came from a small oil lamp with a short wick, which they used sparingly. They ate in that space, slept in that space, and went to the bathroom in that space. At night, usually after 11 PM, Herschel would climb out of the hole to straighten up. Ruchel would often go days without coming out, too fearful that any sound would be heard, and would give them away. Malka, the two-year-old toddler, had only the whispered voices of her parents, and the mice and insects to amuse her. Every week, on Saturday nights, they all ventured into the farmhouse for an hour or so, to wash, change their clothes, and breathe fresh air.

The foreman of the flourmill where Herschel had worked, a rich and generous Czech, was the only other person, besides the farmer, who knew where they were hiding. This man, Lusick Babushkin, was one of the many brave non-Jews who risked their own lives so that they may save others. Lusick did what he could to make their miserable existence more tolerable. He made sure that Herschel, Ruchel, and Marilyn never knew hunger. He brought them meat, butter, bread, and milk, all treasured commodities in the war ravaged region, even for those not in hiding.

As they sat in the darkness, they knew nothing about the war. They only persisted, day-after-day, with the hope that patience would bring some reward. Herschel reached many low points, but Ruchel kept him optimistic. "Do this for your daughter," she implored him. Many people did not take the risk of bringing infants and toddlers into hiding. Many Jews did the unthinkable. They drowned or suffocated their babies, knowing that the children could never survive in hiding, or that the children's screams and cries would lead to the discovery and death for all those in the hiding place. Their child was their life, however, and Ruchel and Herschel would have it no other way. But Herschel truly did not believe they would survive. He eventually resigned himself. "There is always time to die. What can we lose by staying here one more day?"

They lived their silent life in the hole for sixteen months. In the winter of 1944, the farmer summoned Herschel. It was daytime. He had never approached them during the day before. "Come out here. I want you to hear something." Herschel warily emerged. Was it a trick? Were the Ukrainians or the Nazis waiting for him? It was the first time he had seen daylight in sixteen months. He squinted in the light, his eyes burning from adjustment from the dark. Herschel looked around, and realized that there was no one to arrest him. They listened as the sound of Russian artillery exploded in the distance. "They are fifty kilometers from here," the farmer informed him.

One week later, the Soviet army liberated Ozeryany. Ruchel, Herschel, and Malka emerged from the bunker. The farmer took them, by horse and cart, about twenty kilometers to the nearest main town. They saw three Red Army soldiers standing in the main square. Herschel walked up to the soldiers. One of the three, a lieutenant, was a woman. She spoke to him.

"You are liberated."

Herschel just stood there in disbelief.

"You are Jewish?" the lieutenant asked him.

"Yes," he answered.

"How did you survive?" she asked, sympathetically.

Herschel pointed to the farmer, who was still standing only a few steps away.

The lieutenant walked to the farmer and shook hands with him.

"Thank you for your help," she told him.

Herschel quickly realized the lieutenant was Jewish.

"Can you help us?" Herschel asked.

"Tell me what you need," the lieutenant shot back.

"We need a place to live."

The lieutenant gave him a note to take to a man at a building in the town that had been a Jewish hotel before the war. When they arrived at the hotel, it was intact, and full of available, furnished rooms. They had their pick—and picked the nicest room. Within days, the few Jewish survivors from all over the area began arriving at the hotel. They began sharing their horrific and miraculous stories, and making connections to reunite family members.

It was through this network that Songa learned Ruchel and Herschel were alive. The news stunned Songa, offering an unexpected reprieve from the bleakness that had become his existence. The rest of his family, Songa's Uncles Morris and Julius, in the United States, and an uncle and aunt in Palestine, were all tragically unaware of the devastation to their family and their home.

◆　　◆　　◆

With nothing left but his life as a soldier, Songa returned to his troops at the front line, now pushing westward toward Germany. While victory was in the air, the Germans still fought the Soviets with every last bit of strength they had. The number of casualties on both sides was still significant. But with the continuous Allied air attacks successfully destroying all of the weapon-making capability in Germany, and the continued erosion of the strength of German manpower, the capture of Berlin seemed imminent.

On December 31,1944, Stalin recognized the Polish Committee of National Liberation as the Provisional Government of Poland, seemingly sealing Poland's post-war fate as a Communist country under his control. Seventeen days later, Songa participated in the liberation of Warsaw, a major victory for which he later received a medal of honor. But it was a bitter victory for Songa, one that left him with deep conflicted feelings of his role, and an uncomfortable window into the politics of this war.

The liberation of Warsaw, the most significant symbol of the end of the Nazi occupation of Poland, was tinged with controversy and tragedy. In August 1944, four months before the Soviet and its satellite Polish Army finally marched into Warsaw, an attempt to overthrow the Nazi occupiers was made by the underground Polish Home Army. The non-Communist Polish army mounted its rebellion with the expectation that the Red Army, positioned on the outskirts of the city, would bring backup reinforcement. Because of the murky politics, Stalin commanded his forces not to move in and help the Home Army. He had not yet sealed the future territorial conditions and establishment of his Communist government, and he was unwilling to allow the popular Home Army, keepers of the dream of an independent Poland, to claim victory for the people of Poland.

The result was a disastrous sixty-three days of fighting, ultimately ending in the Nazi defeat of the Home Army. Warsaw was virtually destroyed. Nazi soldiers methodically burned and dynamited buildings, leaving a sea of rubble and carnage. More than 250,000 people were killed as a result of the drawn out fighting, the majority of them civilian Poles. Songa, flooded with memories of the beautiful and bustling Warsaw he experienced as a teenager, had been forced to watch the carnage and destruction helplessly from the sidelines, commanded to stay put, rather than to move in and overtake the German troops. He was disgusted by the politics that had caused the needless death and destruction.

◆　　◆　　◆

The final assault on the Germans had begun in February 1945. Their army was on the run, westward, and the Polish and Soviet forces pushed rapidly toward the Oder River, that today represents part of the border between Germany and Poland. Even though the Nazis were in full retreat, the fighting remained fierce, and casualties continued to mount.

Songa reached German soil as the winter of 1945 turned into spring. His first stop was in the town Schneidemuhl, about seventy-five miles east of the Oder River, near Leipzig. He was no longer reclaiming occupied territory; he was now the occupier, surrounded by German civilians whom Songa deemed to be as guilty as their family members in uniform. It was here that he instructed his men to knock on the doors of houses in search of Jewish survivors. "If you find any Jews, bring them to me," he commanded. House-by-house, Songa's men went, knocking on doors, storming into the homes of terrified Germans.

In one house they found a man who had just emerged from hiding, and the soldiers brought him to Songa. When he appeared before Songa, the lieutenant with the Polish Army, the man trembled with fear. Songa put his hand firmly on the man's shoulder and spoke to him in Yiddish.

"Are you Jewish?" he asked. The man stood before him and nodded, cautiously.

"So am I," Songa continued. The man stood before Songa, dumbfounded.

"You look like you don't believe me, so I will show you." Songa proceeded to pull down his uniform trousers to show the man he was circumcised. The man's eyes filled with weary tears of disbelief.

"You are safe now," Songa said quietly, his voice choking. "Let me know if I can do anything for you," he said as he turned to leave. Both men knew that the war was effectively over.

As Songa moved through the German towns and villages on the way to Berlin, he continued to seek out Jewish survivors. He did what he could for them, using his considerable authority to provide them with basic provisions as well as sought-after food. He had seen enough death, and now he became consumed with the living.

While Songa turned his attention from the killing and hatred of German soldiers, to finding Jewish survivors and saving as many lives as possible, many of the Soviet Polish Army and Red Army soldiers were on the rampage for vengeance. The easiest targets for their hatred of the Nazis were the German women left behind in the small towns outside Berlin. Marshall Zhukov, the lionized commander of the Red Army, actually offered the spoils of war as an incentive to his troops. Soviet soldiers, who took control of a German city or town, were officially allowed to have several days to run wild. The soldiers shamelessly raped the German women and looted the towns. Songa would have no part of it. He watched the plundering and the rape with disgust. He prided himself on never touching a German woman, not so much because of high morals, but rather, because his hatred for the Germans was so intense that he could not envision denigrating himself by touching the body of a German woman.

By April, he had reached the shores of the Elbe River, about sixty miles outside Berlin. It was here that he saw, for the first time, the faces of his allies. After literally walking thousands of miles over the course of four years, Soviet forces were now within steps of American soldiers. They waved to each other like long lost family. Songa, who spoke no English, shared a cigarette with an American soldier while sitting on the riverbank. It was an extremely emotional interaction, yet not a word was exchanged. Both men knew that their shared moment was truly symbolic of their victory. But victory, however palpable, would still exact a toll.

The Americans and British would watch while the Soviets were given the *honor* of marching into Berlin. It would prove to be a dubious honor: the Battle of Berlin became one of the bloodiest battles of the war, taking the lives of another 100,000 Soviet soldiers. It had to be fought house-by-house, street-by-street, as the Nazis were determined to hold out until the bitter end.

Songa broke into the city of Berlin, on April 21, 1945, just two months shy of the fourth anniversary of the Nazi invasion of the Soviet Union. In the course of the four years, he had traversed the massive expanse of the Soviet Union and Poland. He now stood in the inner city of Berlin. It was a moment he truly never believed would come.

As the Russians encircled the city, the German soldiers tried to slip to the west, into the American controlled territory. To be captured by the American forces was far more preferable than to surrender to the Red Army soldiers, thirsty for revenge for the devastation of their homeland. The Nazi instinct was correct, at least in Songa's case. Even in those final days of war, he was still a *take no prisoners* officer. Songa overlooked the rules of surrender, and continued to make sure that every German soldier falling into his hands was shot.

On April 30, 1945, Hitler committed suicide. On May 2, the few remaining Nazi fighters trying to hold the streets of Berlin surrendered to the Soviets. The official unconditional surrender came on May 9, 1945.

The war was over, and the Soviets were in control of Berlin. Four years of fighting had passed, and Songa, much to his own disbelief, was alive to see the end. He had never allowed himself to plan for this moment, but he knew instinctively what he wanted to do as soon as he received word of the final surrender.

He made his way to what was left of the bombed German Chancellery. The Reichstag building was newly covered with the flag of the Soviet Union. Here, against the building that had housed the Nazi government—the building in which Hitler and his top officials of the Third Reich systematically planned the annihilation of his Jewish brethren—Songa dropped his pants and attempted to defecate on the ruins. Unfortunately, nature did not cooperate with the intended expression of his sentiments. He settled for urinating on the building instead. "I am pissing on your grave, you dirty bastards," he hissed to himself.

The vodka flowed, and the celebratory gunfire rang through the air, but Songa, and everyone else, knew the celebration was bittersweet. Hitler had been defeated, fascism suppressed, and good conquered evil. While the other Allies celebrated a victory for democracy, the Soviets celebrated the victory of their war of Communism against Fascism.

But while the future generations of so many families were given peace and stability through the defeat of the Germans, other families, completely extinguished, would never produce future generations. Until the day he died, Songa would associate the calendar days with his experiences during the war: where he was, what battle was being fought, who was dying, even what the weather was like that day. He remembered the dates and events in vivid detail, never able to put the horror of World War II behind him.

7

Life After Death

The war was over. Millions of soldiers returned to civilian life, and the challenge of rebuilding new lives for themselves. But Songa, seeing no life to return to, stayed in uniform. There was nothing left for him back in Ozeryany. His family was gone. He had no civilian profession to return to. There was no one and no thing for which he was responsible. He was alone.

What he did have was his increasing power and command in the Polish army, an army that was mobilizing to take on a strong role in post-war Eastern Europe. He used his military career to fill the void left by the war. It gave him a home, a community, a sense of order, and purpose in an otherwise senseless world.

Songa was a Jew in post-war Poland, but he was not a *survivor* according to the societal definition at the time. Survivors had experienced the war in concentration camps or in hiding. Jewish survivors were the people wandering nomadically through post-war Europe, moving through the confused world of Displaced Person's camps, many of which were refashioned concentration camps, trying to reestablish their humanity and their place in the world. Songa had some measure of control over his life. After all, in uniform, Songa was an important man. He had earned no less than six medals for heroic service in the war. In post-war Europe, where chaos abounded as Jews and non-Jews tried to pick up the pieces of their former lives, Songa was one of the people in charge. *He* was giving the orders. *He* was positioned to be a part of the reconstruction of an orderly and civilized existence for the masses of people left with nothing.

Songa could only go so far, however, in using the cloak of his uniform to escape from his own devastating reality. All he had to do was look at the faces of the people for whom he was rebuilding. Before the war, Poland contained one of the largest Jewish populations in the world, second only to the United States. One-third of the country's urban population had been Jewish. Now, the Jews were gone, annihilated, or refugees, who uniformly wanted nothing to do with their homeland. The Jewish refugees, with their Displaced Persons status, did whatever they could to move out of the Soviet-controlled territory, and into either the American or British zones. In the American or British zones, they could believe that a better life might be in their future.

It was the Poles who were left in Poland, the Poles, many of whom were less than sympathetic to the Jews, allowing historic anti-Semitic attitudes to resurface as soon as their common enemy—the Germans—had disappeared. It was the Poles who stood in the ruins of their towns and cities, who hated the Communists and their manipulated takeover of the formerly independent Poland, and who may even have blamed the Jews for their current plight. Stripped of their pre-war independence, passed from German occupation to Soviet occupation, the Polish citizens rightfully questioned how they could consider themselves liberated in the post-war world. And Songa, who had ironically benefited so much from a childhood lived under independent Polish rule, was now functioning as an agent of the perceived oppressors, regardless of his personal political beliefs and ideologies.

After spending several months in various Polish cities, Songa was ordered to report to the city of Lublin. Before the war, Lublin had a population of about 122,000 inhabitants, and was known as both an intellectual center, as well as an important center for Jewish culture, serving as home to one of the world's largest yeshivas. In 1944, as the Germans were being pushed out of Poland, Lublin became the seat of Stalin's new Polish government. It had also become a crossroad for Jewish survivors to reunite and search for loved ones. Now, approximately one-and-a-half-years later, Songa was, as he described himself,

"God and Czar," in Lublin. Songa was charged with the task of spending the next year or so piecing the city back together—structurally, psychologically, and most potently, ideologically.

Songa's chosen description of himself as "God and Czar" was earnest in its meaning. To ensure the successful ideological conversion of the region to Stalin's brand of Communism required Songa to have absolute, unquestioned authority. Any insurrection or dissension would not be tolerated. Songa was given orders—directly from the Soviet High Command—to quell any perceived or potential insurgents who could undermine Soviet authority in the region. Political dissidents, Polish nationalists, even the Zionists who stayed to try to organize the few remaining Jews to flee Europe, for Palestine, were all considered potential enemies and a threat to the Communist government. Songa was to be the man who gave the orders to subdue these antagonists. He was the man charged with removing any potential for anti-Communist rebellions.

He had seen enough death and killing. Having to execute the orders to arrest suspected individuals, and put down Polish rebellions, was harder than anything he had to do during the war. Just as Songa had felt watching the hundreds of thousands of Poles die unnecessarily in the Home Army's ill-fated Battle for Warsaw, he again felt very conflicted by the demands of his position in the Communist Polish Army. He came dangerously close to identifying with the insurgents, whose presumed crime was nothing more than the desire to defend their homeland. But, as he had become very adept at doing, he had to divorce his own sentiments from his actions. To act with anything less than full conviction that the spread of Communism was going to save the starving and impoverished Polish people would have jeopardized his career. The NKVD continued to cast its menacing shadow. And these days, his career was all he had. So, with his characteristic single-minded focus, Songa carried out his orders, brilliantly.

Songa found one outlet to alleviate the overbearing pressure of his Lublin command: he could, unlike during the war, be with women again. That is not to say that he did not have his share of wartime affairs. Some who marched alongside him might even suggest that he left his mark in every village he entered, engaging in at least one quick, consensual affair every time the opportunity presented itself. But now, with the war behind him, and with the uniform and the prestige of his position giving him an added boost to his already handsome and commanding presence, Songa could get beyond the fleeting encounters. He sought out as many girlfriends as there were hours to date them.

In the midst of the politics, the poverty, and the destruction, women were his oxygen. He was revived in the company of women. Ensconced in the heart of Poland, Songa, the Zionist shtetl Jew, now found he was enormously attracted to what would previously have been unthinkable back in Ozeryany: the forbidden fruit, the Polish Catholic *shiksa*.

He couldn't keep his hands off the Polish women, their blond hair, blue eyes, and fair skin so unlike the dark-haired, dark-eyed Jewish women, who had always been considered his available pool of dating material. Songa would go to any length for these heavenly creatures. He even tested the malleability of his upbringing so far as to attend church with girlfriends, if he thought it would increase his chances for romance. Sitting next to the girls in church, Songa would smile to himself as he thought of their *sinful* encounters. One girlfriend, who found it particularly difficult to reconcile her faith and her insatiable desire for Songa, managed her guilty pleasures by keeping a crucifix in hand during their lovemaking.

It was during the post-war years that Songa's military career advances seemed boundless. The Soviet High Command continued to be impressed with him, and particularly with his loyal service in Lublin. His performance there earned him a promotion to the rank of captain in August 1946. Early the next year, he was identified as a high potential officer, and was sent to officer training school from March through November of 1947. Soon after completion of this training, in January 1948, Songa was appointed to the highly sensitive and strategically important position of Chief of Intelligence, assigned to the Educational Center of Infantry.

Just a few months later, in March 1948, he became a major, one of the few Jews to hold that rank in the Polish Army. He was, as his family would have said, a big *machers,* an important man in the eyes of the Polish government. Commensurate with his position came the kind of perquisites and privileges that made life very comfortable for him. In post-war Poland, three years after the end of the war, most people were still desperately in need of food and basic goods. Songa, in contrast, had everything he needed. In strictly material terms, he wanted for nothing.

Yet the perquisites and privileges never impressed him. Songa was a simple man, with simple needs, and he had little interest in having things that someone else could not have. He had uncommon self-confidence, and intrinsic motivation, and he did not require external symbols of success to demonstrate his importance. He was famously generous, using his ability to get what were considered luxury items, and to pass on provisions to those he knew were in need. He would arrange to send fabric and other items to the survivors he knew from Ozeryany, enabling them to make clothes and supplement their food supplies.

His rising status did not change his ideology, even as he rose through the ranks and became more, and more of a figure in the Communist-controlled society. With the increased status of his position, and increased importance of his role in the intelligence arena, he was now being invited to attend dinners held for the political elite, moving in higher level Party circles.

He still had much to learn about how to operate in the upper echelons of Stalin's world. When he attended these Party functions, he often had to be reminded by those who knew him well, to "keep his mouth shut," when he started to drink, for fear that his true feelings toward Communism and the government would be revealed. The vodka could potentially prove to be lethal. Songa's closest friends watched him carefully at the official state functions, as he rubbed elbows with people like Nikita Khrushchev, his former commander in the Battle of Stalingrad, fearing that Songa's iconoclastic views might spill out onto unwelcome ears.

8

Through the Iron Curtain

The power, the stimulating career, the plentiful women, and the availability of all of the material goods, did not erase the fact that Songa was still very much alone. The remains of his decimated family were scattered thousands of miles away, in the United States and Palestine.

Ruchel and her family had endured the odyssey of life as Displaced Persons, and had shrewdly managed to head west—traversing Polish, Czech, and Austrian borders, to ultimately cross into Germany and into the safety of the American zone. With brothers living successful lives in America, Ruchel and Herschel held tight to the belief that it would only be a question of when, not if, they would be allowed to emigrate to the United States. They were among the lucky. They had successfully fled the reach of Stalin's oppressive regime.

By 1948, the Eastern European world was becoming more and more insular, with the spread of Communism creating the political fabric for an alienating, and increasingly impenetrable, *Iron Curtain.* Soon Songa would be virtually unable to interact with the outside Western world; he was being taken further and further from any connection to his past.

Along with feeling the effects of Stalin's intention to seal off the Soviet bloc from the rest of the world, by 1948, Songa began to sense the grip of repression tightening inside the borders of the Communist-controlled territory. As much as he believed throughout the war and its immediate aftermath that being Jewish had never led to personal discrimination, Songa now was seeing a dramatic change in the treatment of Jews in the Soviet Union, and in the Communist-controlled regions.

Anti-Semitism was on the rise, not just among the Poles who had never hidden their feelings for the Jews, but at high levels across the Communist Party. Increasingly, anti-Semitism was being condoned, if not fostered, by the Soviet authorities.

Stalin was becoming mistrustful of the Jews. The number of Jews holding high level government positions had dropped precipitously over the past several years. The Soviet Jews had ties to family members abroad, particularly in America, and unwelcome feelings about the newly created state of Israel. In Stalin's mind, these ties presented a significant threat to his fervent promotion of pure nationalist sentiments.

Through his *anti-cosmopolitan* campaign, Stalin began to systematically target the Jewish intellectual community, branding as disloyal many loyal Communists who maintained a secular Yiddish culture rich in literature, music, and the dramatic arts. Many prominent Jews disappeared. Songa could not ignore what was happening, or its implications for his own career and aspirations.

◆   ◆   ◆

It was a casual trip to a Warsaw café in 1948 that would unexpectedly shape Songa's future. While in the café, Songa overheard a group of young Polish soldiers talking at the next table, the volume of their conversation increasing as they continued to throw back the drinks. Songa took interest as one of the young men recounted a recent trip he had taken to America.

Permission to travel outside the Soviet bloc these days was extremely difficult to procure. Travel to America was almost impossible. Songa listened intently as the soldier explained how he had relatives in the United States who had left him an inheritance. He had managed to convince the Polish government to allow him to claim the money in America and return to Poland, rich with his American dollars. The soldier went on to dazzle his companions with stories of his trip.

Songa sat perfectly still as the young men went about their merriment. Hours later, he left the café, armed with a plan that would alter the course of his life in ways unimaginable to those trapped behind Stalin's Iron Curtain. He, too, was determined to get to America.

Songa had had no contact with his relatives in the United States after the war, but he did know through Ruchel and Herschel that they had some measure of financial means. Compared to the impoverished Poles, his relatives were extremely wealthy, and he knew, if presented in the right context, that the allure of wealthy American connections, and the possibility of bringing U.S. dollars into the Polish economy could be very appealing to the government. Combining the potential stream of American money to the Polish government, with the military intelligence potential of a trip to America by the high ranking intelligence officer, Songa set out to convince the Polish government that he should go to the United States.

To inject some sense of urgency into his petition to the government, Songa, inspired by the experience in the Warsaw café, fabricated an intricate story of an inheritance that had been left by a wealthy relative—a Baron in title—on his father's side. As the only surviving member of his family, Songa argued, he was the rightful heir to the money, a substantial fortune that could only be claimed in person, in America. He was reasonably secure in his lie, believing that he could come up with the necessary money from his relatives to substantiate his fabricated inheritance.

He proposed to travel to the U.S. on official business, as a military attaché of the Polish Army, claim his inheritance, gather intelligence, develop contacts in the United States through his network of relatives, and return to Poland. To accomplish this, he requested a three-month visa.

The plan was appealing to the Polish authorities. Songa was one of their rising stars, and his loyalty to his position and the army had been proven time and again. His commitment to his military career was further demonstrated by the fact that he had recently been accepted to the prestigious Academy of Voroshilov in Moscow. The Academy was the premiere Red Army officer training academy, intended for elite, high ranking officers who wanted to become the Army's future leaders. Songa, having already accomplished so much by the age of thirty-two, had now set his sights on reaching the highest military position in one of the largest and strongest armies in the world. According to his stated plans, he would, upon his return from the United States, move from Poland to Moscow to attend the Academy.

Still, the government did not grant permission to cross the impenetrable Iron Curtain without some guarantees. Songa's commanding officer and others in key positions of authority were more than willing to vouch for his intentions, and offered themselves as collateral for his return. This man was no defector. This man was no traitor. So confident were they in the words, distinguished career, and commitment of Major Ajces that these high-ranking Communist officers agreed to jeopardize their own careers, and even their lives, to allow Songa to travel to America.

Once he had committed himself to the plan by publicly presenting his case, Songa became obsessed with seeing it successfully executed. Getting to America became his only goal, replacing everything else that he had thought was important. It became, simply, his reason for being.

The background work to master the logistics necessary to execute Songa's plan took months of planning. Songa had to work both ends of the bureaucracy; once he obtained permission to leave, at least in theory, from the Polish government, he needed to secure permission from the United States government to enter, an almost impossible feat with Cold War tensions festering.

Communication between the Western world and the Eastern world was difficult, slow, and censored. Songa knew all written communication sent and received passed under the eyes of the Communist government, and he always kept his letters brief and business-like. He knew not to put anything in writing that might ever serve to incriminate him. He had woven an intricate fabrication, and had to exercise mighty caution to ensure there were no missteps. Songa had survived the NKVD once. Once was enough to be forever meticulous.

Songa knew no English, spoken or written, and was entirely dependent on his American family to execute the details with the United States government on his behalf. The primary American contacts were his second cousins, the Berkule family. He used Ruchel's husband Herschel, now living in a Displaced Persons camp in Germany, as an intermediary. Songa wrote to Herschel, and Herschel wrote to the American cousins to apprise them of Songa's plans and to enlist their help.

Songa's second cousin, Leon Berkule, had been born in Ozeryany, and while still an infant, left with his four sisters, a brother, and his mother and father, in the late 1920s. Leon was only three years older than Songa. They were both named Lazar, and even though they had never met in person, they shared a bond that would grow remarkably strong over time. Leon Berkule was a young attorney, and by default, became the designated representative of the American relatives. He would manage all of the complex interactions necessary in the attempt to get Songa to the United States. Fortunately for Songa, the Berkules had resources and connections. Affidavits had to be signed, money had to be sent, and endless paperwork had to be completed from the American end.

By August of 1948, Songa's request for travel was approved, and a three-month visa to travel to the United States was granted. In October, the visa was in his hand, effective immediately. With the clock ticking, he still needed a mode of transport to the United States. He was traveling on official government business, but the Polish government was not prepared to either fund or facilitate his transport.

Songa soon learned that he could get passage to New York City on the Polish passenger ship, the *SS Batory*. Leon Berkule had sent $250 in American money to cover the cost of the passage. That was the good news. The bad news was that he learned of the next sailing opportunity less than twenty-four hours before the *Batory* was scheduled to depart.

After months and months of planning, he now had just hours to pack and prepare for the trip. After nine years of waiting, harkening back to his restless days in 1939, when he wanted to see the world and travel to New York City to attend the World's Fair, Songa now had only hours before he would depart.

With so little time, he hurriedly threw together some belongings, giving little consideration to what he should bring. What artifacts of his life could he bring to help his American relatives understand what he and his family had endured? He grabbed some photographs and left it at that. Everything would be searched anyway.

Songa made his way, small suitcase in hand, to the Polish port city of Gdynia where the *Batory* was docked. On a cold, gray, October 25, 1948, in full dress uniform, covered by a floor-length black overcoat, Songa stepped onto the ship, ready to leave the continent of Europe for the first time in his life. He prepared himself for the long journey to America.

The *SS Batory* was one of the newer ships in the Gdynia-America line, finished in 1936 for transatlantic trade and passengers. During the war, the *Batory* had fallen into American hands, and at the conclusion of the war, went back to the Poles primarily for North Atlantic maritime trade. When Songa boarded the ship in 1948, it had just undergone a refit, and everything was sparkling and fresh. For the young man unaccustomed to any travel outside the Soviet-controlled system, the *Batory* seemed like the height of luxury. He traveled as a first-class passenger. He unpacked his sparse belongings and settled into his large, comfortable stateroom.

As the ship departed, Songa was filled with feelings he had not known since he was a child—heightened anticipation, excitement, and a sense of wonder. He had never been at sea, and stepped out onto the deck, soaking in the salty air, the rocking motion, and the vast emptiness for as far as the eye could see. He thought about arriving in New York City, a place he had only read about and seen in the movies, unable to imagine that in a few weeks time he would be seeing it and experiencing it up close.

As the ship moved farther and farther from the port, Songa was overwhelmed by the strange sense of freedom he felt, knowing that he would soon be crossing outside the boundaries of the tightly sealed Communist region. And then, he was flooded with thoughts of his reunion with family members, who, while distant in many ways, were his only connection to a past that had been otherwise completely erased by the war. In the faces of his uncles and cousins, he might see his own parents, his grandmother, his brother and sister. In America, it might be possible to resurrect the ghosts of everyone whom he had loved and lost.

The ship made two stops en route to America, first in Copenhagen, and then in Southampton. His reception at these port stops foreshadowed many things to come. Neither the Danish nor the British wanted anything to do with this high-ranking officer in the Communist Polish Army, and he was not permitted to get off the ship at either port.

From Southampton, it was on to New York. The autumn Atlantic seas were particularly rough and stormy in 1948, and the crossing made most of the passengers violently ill and unable to do more than nurse their seasickness in their cabins. Songa was one of only two passengers who proved impervious to the bumpy seas: he was the only one who made it to every meal in the ship's dining room. If he had the constitution to withstand starvation and torture in a Soviet political prison and stay healthy and alive through the fiercest battles of WWII, bumpy seas were not going to keep him down.

After twelve days at sea, on November 6, 1948, the *SS Batory* reached the shores of America and pulled into Pier Fifty-four in midtown Manhattan. Songa drew a deep breath, partly to confirm that he was, in fact, awake and not hallucinating, as he prepared to disembark. He was eager to stand on land again, after two weeks at sea. He did not know it, but the entire contingency of New York relatives, numbering almost twenty people, came to the ship to greet him. Most of them had heard only the apocryphal stories about this hero of the war, one of the only family members to survive the remote war they had only experienced second-hand.

Songa prepared emotionally for what lay before him. It was going to be particularly difficult to reunite with Julius and Morris Feinblatt, his two uncles who had left Ozeryany for New York City when Songa was still a boy. As times became more and more difficult back in Ozeryany in the 1930s, Songa always believed these two men did not extend help to their mother or their siblings back home. Songa, whose nature at the core was to help people if one had the ability, was always very disturbed by what he considered the selfish actions of these uncles. But he would suppress those feelings, for the moment, in order to make this a happy reunion.

As he began to disembark, his entrance onto American soil hit an unexpected impasse. Rather than strolling down the gangway into the eagerly awaiting arms of American cousins, Songa was greeted in New York City by immigration officials. They had taken one look at his papers and decided this Major Ajces, of the Soviet-controlled Communist Polish Army, was not the most desirable visitor to New York. They would not let Songa disembark from the ship.

Virtually all of the passengers had disembarked. Leon Berkule, who stood among the anxious family members, sensed something had gone wrong, and he used his status as an attorney to talk his way past the guards to board the ship. The lower deck was all but abandoned. Leon found his cousin wandering on the deck, dressed in his uniform, looking as imposing as a major in the Polish Army should look. And yet, as imposing as the uniform and the appearance of this cousin was, Leon noticed that Songa looked just a little bit lost—a little bit wide-eyed—wandering aimlessly and trying to figure out what was happening. Leon approached him and simply said, in Yiddish, "You must be Songa." The two men embraced. Songa was in America.

Songa was, more accurately, in American waters, as he was not permitted on land. Officials ferried him straight to Ellis Island for detention as a suspicious person, until his situation could be investigated further. Even with all of the advanced planning, paperwork, affidavits, and effort, the United States was still not quite sure about the wisdom of allowing this Communist military intelligence officer onto American soil. Leon Berkule spoke to him in Yiddish, trying to assure him that they would take care of the situation. Songa, in the meantime, could do nothing but comply.

Ellis Island, as a transition point to the brave new world, did not seem too forbidding to Songa. In fact, he felt reasonably comfortable, with decent food, a place to shower, and a small room to himself for sleeping. By comparison to a detention center in the Soviet Union, Ellis Island could almost pass for a hotel. The worst part of his two days on Ellis Island was the boredom of being holed up there, coupled with the anticipation of whether he would actually be allowed to stay in America. Songa, who was always in perpetual motion, was restless. He spoke no English, and therefore, could communicate with no one. Among the entertainment available at Ellis Island, was, oddly enough, a ping-pong table. That ping-pong table proved to be Songa's salvation, as he played game after game in wordless competition to pass the time and to keep his mind off his troubles.

Two nights passed on Ellis Island, and on November 8, 1948, Leon arrived at Ellis Island to claim his cousin. The family had to post a $500 bond as security that Songa would not become a "ward of the United States." Otherwise, he was free to go, released into his cousin's custody. They went directly to the home of Leon's sister, Clara, in Jackson Heights, Queens. Sitting in the back seat of the car as they drove across the Triborough Bridge from Manhattan to Queens, Songa said little. Finally, roughly three weeks after he had left Poland, Songa stood firmly on American soil.

The Berkules, originally Berkowitz, had left Ozeryany for America long before the war, and these cousins were culturally foreign to Songa. They had been raised as Americans in New York City. They ate American food. They amused themselves with American pastimes and entertainment. They spoke English like New Yorkers. But assimilation hadn't completely taken away their Ozeryany roots, and Yiddish was spoken equally with English in the Berkule home.

Songa was very shy and withdrawn in those first few hours among his American family. But he was able to quickly bond with his cousins in the one language they had in common. Being able to communicate with anyone in this foreign country was welcome, but conversing in Yiddish with these strangers, who also happened to be his family, filled Songa with bittersweet warmth, turning back the clock to remind him of how much he had lost, and how much was missing from his life in the army.

The Berkules treated him like visiting royalty. With the comforts bestowed upon him from his overly doting family, and the simple comforts of life in America in the late 1940s, Songa started to settle in to life in New York City during the closing months of 1948. And while the availability of food, goods, and services made less of an impression on him than one would think, given that he lived his life in war-ravaged Eastern Europe, New York City itself made an enormous impression on the thirty-two-year-old army major.

He found walking the streets of Manhattan electrifying, and when he strolled Broadway and the theater district, the marquees pulsing in their high wattage glory, he remained in a constant state of stupefied amazement. He thought Central Park was a treasure, the abundance of neatly landscaped nature right in the heart of the city, and he explored it from end to end. He roamed the grand halls of the New York Public Library and read Polish and Yiddish language periodicals in the European Reading Room. But the part of New York City that made him really appreciate what the modern democratic world was all about was the subway. The fast, efficient, and egalitarian movement of thousands of people across hundreds of miles of track every day enthralled the strategic and logistically minded military officer. Some days he would ride the subways for hours on end, studying the map, listening to the conversations, watching, and learning.

Living in New York City, was, however, far from a wide-eyed adventure filled with excitement and possibility. Songa was very mindful of who he was in the eyes of the American government and the American people. His survival instinct told him it would be best to "keep his mouth shut." Fortunately, this did not pose too much hardship. He had no ability to communicate in English, anyway. He felt like he was being watched in those early days in New York City, and in fact, he was being scrutinized by the FBI. They were tracking his every movement, covertly and overtly.

Several times during his stay in Jackson Heights, a team of FBI agents showed up at Clara's door, demanding to speak with him. The men would disappear into the bedroom of the small apartment and interview him for hours. Without a doubt, his presence was considered a threat in the increasingly Communist-paranoid country. The FBI was determined to understand him: What was his real purpose in coming to America? Who was he meeting with? Where was he traveling?

Songa had his standard script, which he echoed in each interrogation. But by the time of his third and fourth interrogations, he had already absorbed what it meant to live in America. America, he now understood, was a place where ordinary citizens could voice their opinions about politics and policies, where anyone could seek an education or strive for a better life, where individuals had rights to privacy and the government did not control their every action.

The small taste of life in this country had already had a significant impact on Songa. The freedom he had experienced made it increasingly difficult to stick to his standard script in answering the FBI's questions. He was forced to question his motives. "What was his real purpose in coming to America?" he thought to himself.

Time passed too quickly, and two months had already slipped by. Leon Berkule felt that he had built enough of a relationship with Songa to ask what seemed like terribly obvious questions to the American: "Why are you going back to Poland?" "There's nothing there for you." "What kind of a life could you possibly have there, with no family and no political freedom?" "How can you pass up all of the possibilities and opportunities waiting for you here in America?" These questions soon became a relentlessly loud and repetitive chorus from all of the Berkule cousins.

Songa, seemingly resolute in his conviction that his place was back in the army, attempted to explain to his cousins the status and stature of his position in the military, and his career aspirations to rise even higher in the army. He told them of his plans to enter the Academy of Voroshilov. But the conversation always went nowhere, as the Americans could never understand Songa's motivation to rise and serve under such a repressive regime.

To Americans, Stalin was the enemy. The fact that Songa had a very important position and what he considered to be a relatively good life in Poland was meaningless to them. Moreover, Songa was, out of necessity, tight-lipped about the politics of the situation, and the American cousins failed to fully appreciate the implications of a fanatically controlled Polish government eagerly awaiting the return of one its senior military officers. Not to return would have severe, if not fatal, consequences for Songa as well as for all of the trusting friends and officials that put their lives on the line to allow him to leave Poland.

His relatives continued to hound Songa, imploring him to violate the visa, set to expire on the fast approaching date of January 25, 1949. They went so far as to engage the services of a prominent immigration lawyer. "Seek political asylum and stay in the United States, Songa," they begged. "Don't be foolish." The cousins were dumbfounded by what seemed to be his unflappable loyalty to a Communist regime. They were seeing the effects of Songa's years of Red Army training and had no context to interpret his behavior. They had no understanding of what his life had been like, of what it meant to come of age in war, and to devote a career to the unquestioning fulfillment of the maniacal aspirations of a dictator.

But his family's relentless effort to get him to stay in America was not falling on deaf ears. Songa had had a taste of freedom. He knew, in his heart, that he could never go back. And he admitted privately that he was never completely sure of what happened to him on that day, in the café in Warsaw, when he resolved to seek his visa in the first place. Perhaps he never intended to return.

There was no one who was less of a Communist by nature or ideology than Songa, and as he began to believe in the possibilities life could offer him in the capitalist, democratic environment of America, he started to publicly waver on his steadfast resolve to go back. The hustle and bustle of New York City slowly reawakened the long dormant entrepreneurial spirit that had so long ago compelled the seventeen-year-old Songa to start a bicycle business. And while the clock ticked toward January 25, and his life-altering decision would have to be made soon, the family received news.

Ruchel and Herschel had finally been granted permission to immigrate to the United States. After living for almost four years in the DP camps, they would be able to create an American home for themselves. Songa could be reunited with his aunt. Ruchel was the only other person from his family who understood the pain and suffering of the war. She was his *tante* with whom he had shared his childhood, who took care of his sister Rose when she became ill, who sang Russian folk songs in her beautiful, clear voice while he accompanied her on the mandolin. This would be his only chance to see her.

Ruchel and Herschel had saved their daughter Malka, one of the few children brought to the DP camp, an excruciatingly painful reminder that more than one million Jewish children living in Poland were murdered during the war. Furthermore, Ruchel and Herschel had gone on to do the unthinkable: they decided, as homeless refugees, to have another child in post-war Europe, and their son Matthew was born in the DP camp in Germany. For Songa, Ruchel and Herschel were the symbol of life—of the continuity of Eastern European Jewry. Now, in just two months, the four of them would be arriving in the United States to start anew.

The contours of Songa's decision-making were now radically reshaped. After all these years, after all of the bloodshed, Songa and Ruchel could be together again. This was his closest family. This would be his only opportunity to see her. How could he walk away from that reunion and return to Poland, potentially cut off from the Western world for years to come? Suddenly, nothing else mattered. Even the threat to his life and the lives of those who trusted him in Poland seemed distant.

Hitler failed to annihilate all of the Jews of Europe, as he intended. Songa had seen the mass graves, the crematoriums, but he was alive now to talk about it, and to document the atrocities. Songa had survived. Ruchel and Herschel and their children had survived. Their legacy would live on for generations to come, and Songa suddenly understood that he needed to be a part of it. With Ruchel, he had a chance to begin the healing process from the trauma of the war, to resurrect his former self, to feel joy again, and to mourn properly for all that was lost. Now it was time. Songa made the decision to seek political asylum, to defect. He wanted to live in America. Major Lazar Ajces, of the Communist Polish Army was set to reinvent himself as the civilian New Yorker, Leon Ajces.

9

My Name is Leon Ajces

Songa's decision to defect equated to a self-imposed death sentence from the Polish government, for their major in charge of the Third Infantry Division, and former senior intelligence officer. The moment he violated his visa, he knew he could never go back.

The finality of the consequences of his decision from the Polish end was clear. What was far less certain was the reception on the part of the United States government to his request for political asylum. His chilly reception from the Immigration and Naturalization Services (INS) upon his arrival in New York, and the ensuing FBI monitoring gave him little reason to be optimistic. As an intelligence officer from a Communist army, his case would be extremely difficult to prove. It would be subject to the highest level of scrutiny and would require great persuasive powers and evidence to show that his defection motivations were genuine, and not merely crafted as a ploy to remain as a spy in America.

Compounding the intense pressure he felt from the uncertainty of his fate, were the other challenges as well: the daily challenges of assimilating to life as a defector in America. Songa spoke five languages, but English was not one of them. He had spent the last decade, virtually all of his adult life, in the army, where life was programmed for him, and he would now have to adjust to civilian life. He was used to barking orders; now he would no longer be the man in charge. He would suddenly find himself at the bottom of the rung of New York City immigrant life—an immigrant arriving with few possessions, who did not speak the language, and who hailed from a Communist country increasingly viewed as the enemy.

With the well-connected Berkules working on his political asylum case, enlisting the help of one the best-known immigration lawyers in New York City, there was little for Songa to do on his own behalf. He became increasingly frustrated with his inability to communicate outside of the Yiddish-speaking community. He was unaccustomed to having no responsibilities. It had been the first time he had slowed down since 1939, before the war had started. He was bored, anxious, impatient, and doubting his decision. As he obsessively reviewed the potential consequences of his decision to defect—for himself as well as for those back in Poland who had vouched for him—he slipped further and further into a depressive episode.

He spent January and February of 1949 in bed. Songa slept all day, staying in bed day-after-day, emerging sometimes late in the afternoon, only to eat a few bites before retreating back to the bedroom. The Berkules began to worry about his condition, but Songa would not communicate and would not allow them to seek help. Songa's Uncle Julius looked in on him one day, as he lay in the darkened room, and said with disgust, "You are a lazy good-for-nothing. You will never amount to anything in this country."

He hated what he had become. Songa had no tolerance for weakness—in himself or in others. He didn't believe in doctors, and he certainly would never consider professional counseling. Intensely private, and unwilling to share his thoughts with others, Songa simply resolved to shake himself out of the psychological paralysis, as if through sheer force of will he could cure himself of whatever it was that took hold of him after his defection.

He forced himself to think positively. "I will remain in this country," he told himself over-and-over again. "I will make a life for myself." And slowly, he began to lay the groundwork for his new life in America.

He took small steps, things that were within his control. He started by making a list of what he needed to do: change his name, move to his own place, learn English, and get a job. The first task would be the most emblematic—to take an English name, and to proclaim his new American identity. Lazar became Leon, the same name as his cousin Leon, and while he remained Songa to family and close friends throughout his life, to the outside world he was now Leon Ajces.

He moved out of Clara's house in Jackson Heights to gain some measure of privacy and independence. The Berkules secured a room for him in Manhattan, at the residential Ansonia Hotel on Manhattan's Upper Westside. Now he was no longer in the outer boroughs of New York City, but directly in the heart of the city. It was here that he could feel inspired by the daily pulse of city life.

Most importantly, he needed to find work. He had no money of his own, and to continue to live off the generosity of the Berkules was unacceptable to this intensely proud man. Work also represented his lifeline: he had to demonstrate to the American government, as part of his political asylum request, that he would be a self-supporting contributor to the American economy, and not a drain on the country's resources. The United States government had no use for defectors who were needy in any way. Any work at all would be better than being idle.

And he was still acutely aware that the FBI continued to watch his every move.

On March 17, 1949, the last remnants of Songa's depression dissipated. On that day, he stood at the pier to greet the arriving ship that had transported Ruchel, Herschel, Malka, and Matthew to New York City. Now Songa held his arms out to Ruchel for the first time since a brief reunion in the war-torn days in Poland, just after the liberation of Ozeryany, and shortly after Songa had learned the emotionally crippling news of his family's fate. In Poland, they had cried endless tears of anguish and suffering. Now they cried plentiful tears of hope, growth, and renewal. Standing at the pier, holding his aunt, and looking at the children's faces, Songa knew that whatever happened with his asylum request, his decision to violate the visa was the right one.

Songa's Uncle Morris had arranged for an apartment in the Bronx for his newly arrived sister and her family. Songa immediately left Manhattan for the Bronx as well, in order to be close to them. He rented a room a few blocks from Ruchel's apartment, off the Grand Concourse, from a Jewish seamstress named Dorothy Glockenberg.

Mrs. Glockenberg was only too happy to take good care of Songa. She spoke Yiddish, and made sure he was well fed. Between Ruchel and Mrs. Glockenberg, his old charm started to return, and he became his playful self again, all the while enjoying the doting attention—just as he had in his childhood home. The Grand Concourse was true to its name, the elegant main thoroughfare of the Bronx, packed with shopping, entertainment, and upscale apartment buildings, attracting many upper middle-class Jewish inhabitants. Songa lived comfortably here as a boarder in the Glockenberg home. He spent countless hours with Ruchel and Herschel, exchanging stories and experiences, catching up on almost ten years of life that had been ripped away from them, once again becoming a family.

While his personal life and living situation were remarkably improved, Songa's work situation remained a disaster. There was no way around the fact that he spoke no English. Demonstrating his extraordinary talents and skills would be impossible; but he was hungry to take any work he could get his hands on.

Through a connection of Clara's husband, Jack, Songa took to the streets of Manhattan's garment district—a haven for low skilled immigrants willing to do any and all kinds of menial labor. Songa's determination to stay in America was strong enough now that he had made peace with the fact that any work was good work, no matter how menial. No honest work would be beneath him. So Songa cleaned bathrooms. He pushed the carts filled with clothes through the streets of the garment district. He worked in a factory. He blocked hats for a milliner. He had uncommon vision and tremendous tolerance for these jobs. Unfortunately, he just couldn't keep a job.

He enlisted his cousin Rose as his interpreter to help him communicate with prospective employers. He was fully aware that he would arouse a healthy dose of suspicion from anyone who might hire him, so Songa tried to resurrect the survival technique that worked for him in his former life, when as a newly liberated NKVD prisoner he was left to wander aimlessly in remote Uzbekistan. Just as he offered his labor in exchange for food, now Songa asked Rose to write a letter for him, in English, that he could hand to a prospective employer:

> "Hire me and don't pay me for two weeks. I'll prove to you how hard I work. At the end of the two weeks, after you see what I can do, you can put me on your payroll."

He walked the streets of Manhattan, the paper on which the note was written becoming tattered from being handed around so often. His tactic was to demonstrate his honesty, earnestness, and his willingness to work hard. Unfortunately, he miscalculated his strategy: the streets of Manhattan were a far cry from the nether regions of Soviet Central Asia, and most of the Garment District's employers at the time had little respect or use for such integrity. Employers usually abused Songa's offer by putting him to work unpaid for the time agreed upon, and then firing him when it came time to put him on the payroll. If he wasn't fired by his bosses, he was muscled out by Unions. In some cases Songa proved too productive, working so quickly that he angered the Union workers who often worked alongside him. He was making them look bad and they wanted him out.

He moved nomadically from job to job, with one episode after another of mistrustful bosses or unwelcoming fellow workers. And yet, it was becoming imperative that he hold on to a job long enough to be convincing in his case for political asylum.

He finally turned, begrudgingly, to his Uncle Julius. Julius had made it in the dry cleaning business. He had three successful stores in Manhattan. Songa appealed to Julius for work. Julius knew his situation, and agreed, reluctantly, to give him a job in one of the stores. But when business got slow, Julius, the same uncle who had proclaimed Songa to be lazy and futureless in America during Songa's early days of defection, told him he could not afford to keep him on the payroll. Julius fired his nephew. Already demoralized by months of failure in the job market, Songa, the man who had achieved so much, the man who had survived the unsurvivable, was starting to feel defeated.

Leon Berkule, who by now had become something of a guardian angel to his cousin Songa, unknowingly came to the rescue. Leon, as a tax attorney, had a client in the publishing distribution business. The client was a company called Novak News, a rough and tumble company in Brooklyn, that acted as the intermediary between the magazine and the book publishers, and the newsstands, where magazines and paperback books were sold. This wholesale publishing business was a world of warehouses and trucks, storing and transporting hundreds of thousands of magazines and books. It was also a world of teamsters and Mafia corruption, and rampant theft.

The business seemed to be a haven for unskilled labor and for immigrants who spoke no English. Leon, through his own dubious business practices, was acting as an interim president for the company; he got his cousin a job sorting books in what was referred to as the book room. The book room was a warehouse space filled with unsold paperback books waiting to be returned to the publisher. All Songa had to do was sort the books into piles as they came in, matching pictures and titles. Nine hours a day, five days a week, Songa sat and sorted. It was the university-educated army major's first steady employment since his arrival in the United States.

Songa revisited the assimilation list that he had plotted out several months earlier. He had changed his name. He had moved out into his own place. He had found steady work. All that remained was the not-so-inconsequential task of learning English. Most of the newly arrived post-war immigrants attended English classes. Songa resisted these classes for no reason other than his genetic impatience; the thought of sitting through those classes with a room full of *schmucks* had no appeal. Ruchel and Herschel, who were studying English nearby, convinced him to attend a class. Songa lasted less than one session. He left the class early, and never returned.

He decided he would teach himself English. He walked the streets of New York with a Polish-English dictionary under one arm, and a Russian-English dictionary under the other. He went to movies. He listened to the radio. He sat on park benches in Central Park, and listened to people talk. He rode the subway. He poured over books in the New York Public Library. And astonishingly, within several months, Leon Ajces, who cursed in Russian and counted in Yiddish, now had a basic understanding of English.

There were, of course, women to keep Songa occupied. This time, however, unlike his love life in post-war Poland, his dating practices became a family affair. Songa was, after all, thirty-three years old, and his family had determined that he should be married. Fixing him up on blind dates became a pastime for his relatives. Songa acquiesced to the set-ups, but only with an elaborate escape route planned in the event that the blind date didn't meet his expectations.

Songa always asked women to meet him at Columbus Circle on the corner of Central Park South and 59th St; he knew there was a phone booth on that corner. He would always arrive early for his dates, perch himself safely across Columbus Circle, and watch as the date arrived to see what she looked like. If he liked what he saw, he would proceed with the date. If he didn't, he would rush up late to meet the unsuspecting prospect, and feign the need to make an urgent phone call from the conveniently located phone booth on the corner. The phone call would always bring bad news, requiring him to break the date. He was a master of deception: The prospective date never understood that she was being *dumped* by her opinionated suitor, her fate determined well before she even exchanged words with him.

But unlike life in uniform in post-war Poland, in America, Songa did not always hold the cards in the dating scene. As handsome and confident as he was, his accent and his status as an immigrant often worked against him among the ladies of New York City, even those with their own Eastern European Jewish roots. For the first time in his life, he suffered punishing rejections from women he courted. These women told him, more often than he would have liked, that they wanted nothing to do with a *foreigner* who couldn't speak English well. Regardless of whom he had once been, Songa was once again reminded of the fact that in New York City, circa 1949, he was climbing up from the bottom rung of the ladder.

As his English improved, so did his ability to demonstrate his considerable intelligence and capabilities. He made work his first priority, and began to move up in responsibility at Novak News. He was a workhorse, and he was getting a very good understanding of the business from the bottom. His hopes for a future in America started to burn a bit brighter, with the satisfaction of earning even a modest living fueling his spirits. But in early fall of that year, the brightness started to dim again.

It was late September 1949, and Songa was thinking about how to celebrate the one-year anniversary of his arrival in America. His thoughts, however, were quickly overshadowed.

The dreaded letter from the United States Department of Immigration and Naturalization Services arrived, dated September 26, 1949. Songa felt sick as he opened the mail and handed it over to Ruchel and Herschel. He did not read English well enough and waited for the translation. From their faces, Songa knew they were reading the equivalent of a warrant for his death. Addressed to Mr. Lazar Ajces, of Bronx, New York, the United States government informed him that his request for the "adjustment of status as a displaced person residing in the United States," had been denied. He was further advised that an "order was being entered to grant you thirty days within which to effect your departure from this country." He was given thirty days to leave the country, thirty days before he would be deposited back into the clutches of Communism and Totalitarianism.

Songa knew he had but one alternative when faced with the threat of deportation. He had just one safety net to pull out as he straddled the politics and bureaucracy, and he knew now was the only chance to use it. If it did not work, he would be dead.

He had come to this country as a military attaché from the Communist Polish Army. He had been a Chief Intelligence officer. Through all his years of directing his men to work to infiltrate the military information systems of perceived enemies, he understood fully how hard the United States was working to infiltrate the seemingly impenetrable Soviet intelligence network. He knew his military intelligence would be highly sought after by the American army. He knew the potential value he presented, and he gambled that the United States would see the value of his knowledge as equal to the value of his life.

Songa was ready to barter his knowledge and experience of the inner workings of the Communist Polish and Red Armies for the rescission of his deportation order. He immediately picked up the phone, called his contacts at the FBI, and asked for a meeting.

Even signaling his willingness to talk, was a self-incriminating action. Six years before, Songa had been wrongfully imprisoned and tortured by the NKVD, under false espionage charges. Now, if his proposal were rejected by the U.S. Army, and indeed he were to be deported, he would have no hope of fighting accusations of espionage in Poland. Cast as a traitor, he would certainly face execution.

He agonized through what seemed like endless days of waiting for a response from the American government. Each night he lay in bed, tormented by the idea that this might be his last night in America, wondering whether this would be his last night of freedom. The answer came only a few days later.

He was at work in the warehouse at Novak News, in Greenpoint, Brooklyn, surrounded by the stacks and stacks of paperback books waiting to be sorted and packaged. The FBI agents appeared at the building. "We are looking for Leon Ajces," they informed the receptionist in the office, as they displayed their badges.

Songa, always an extremely private person, had kept his affairs to himself and his co-workers at Novak knew very little about his immigration issues. Now, Harry Leibowitz and Lester Scherin, the owners of the company, scrambled out of their offices, taking a keen and nervous interest in the FBI's appearance at their office for wholly unrelated reasons. The publishing wholesale business had notorious Mafia ties, and Novak's owners believed they were about to be busted. They waited anxiously to see what the FBI could possibly have wanted with Leon, as the receptionist escorted the agents to the warehouse.

"Let's talk outside," said one of the agents, when they found Songa in the warehouse. The other workers, mostly immigrants themselves with poor English, tried not to show too much interest in the interaction. Songa nodded and led the way, lighting a cigarette as he walked. When they were outside, they talked for some time. At the end of the conversation, Songa understood his future. He was to pack his bags immediately—not for Poland, but for Washington, D.C. The deal was struck, and a plan was in place. They handed Songa a train ticket and some money.

On October 5, little more than a week after he received his initial letter from the INS, another letter from the INS, addressed to Mr. Lazar Ajces, arrived in the Bronx. This letter advised Songa that the agency's previous letter, dated September 26, 1949, "may be disregarded." He was spared, for the moment.

Two weeks later, he left Pennsylvania Station in New York, to head to Washington, D.C. He was to meet with officials from the United States Army, G2 Military Intelligence. Once again, he found himself in transit, small suitcase in hand.

As the train slowly pulled out of the station, Songa closed his eyes and was flooded with the memory of previous train trips to the destinations that forever changed his life: The 1939 train from Ozeryany, that took him to basic training in the Red Army. Next came the 1943 train to Uzbekistan, under arrest by the NKVD. Songa smiled to himself when he thought of the contrast. Unlike those other trips, this time he wasn't filled with dread. This time he was optimistic that his travels would lead him to something better.

He was on his way to the United States Pentagon, about to do what at one time would have been unthinkable for a man who prided himself on his loyalty. He was ready to turn against the country that he knew had long ago betrayed him, in exchange for life in a democracy.

PLEASE REFER TO THIS FILE NUMBER

0300-271148

October 4, 1949

Mr. Lazarz Ajces
c/o Korch, Apt. 1-D
1377 Franklin Avenue
Bronx 56, New York

Dear Sir:

On September 26, 1949, we advised you that an order
had been entered by the Commissioner denying your application
for adjustment of status as a displaced person residing in
the United States. We further advised you that an order was
being entered which would grant you thirty days within which
to effect your departure from this country.

You are notified our letter of September 26, 1949
may be disregarded.

Very truly yours,

TRENT DOSER
Acting District Director
New York District

By

LOYD H. JENSEN
Chief, Expulsion Section

LHJ/con

Songa's great-grandfather,
patriarch of
the Feinblitt family

Songa's parents, Melech and Yetta Ajces

From left to right: Songa (Lazar), Josef, and Rose,
around 1923

Songa's brother, Josef, age 17

Songa, age 21,
with his mother, Yetta.

Songa, far right,
making music with aunts
and cousins, 1929

As lieutenant in the
Polish Army, 1944

Far right with binoculars, Songa taking a rare break during the war

Center, on tank. Songa
with unit, 1942

Songa, far left, with
fellow officers, Poland 1944

In Poland, just after the
war, Songa far left, enjoying
women and cigarettes

In America, Peekskill, NY, 1949. Just after defection, Songa, center, with Uncles Morris and Julius Feinblitt.

As General Manager of Imperial News Company, 1965

October, 1957, Leon and Betty marry in New York City

Betty and Leon, in their first
home, Baldwin, NY, 1961

At the celebration of his 75th birthday,
Garden City Hotel, NY, 1991

Gravestone at
Mount Hebron cemetery,
Flushing, NY

10

Soviet Secrets

Leon arrived in Washington, D.C., in the waning days of 1949, just as Senator Joseph McCarthy mounted the beginning of his crusade against Communism. As Leon soaked up his first glimpse of America's capital city, awestruck as he viewed the mammoth neoclassical buildings that stood as testaments to the ideals of democracy and freedom, McCarthy was twisting and contorting these ideals inside those very buildings, fueling anti-Communist sentiments, and feeding the frenzy of the general paranoia that gripped the nation in the early 1950s.

The United States Army was in the process of committing American troops to a war in Korea, fearful that the Soviets intended to bring the world under Communist control with a systematic program of expansion. Hollywood stars saw themselves blacklisted, careers ruined by rampant accusations of Communist ties. Alleged Communists spies were tried and sentenced to death. And Leon had arrived to work at the Pentagon, ready to bring fact-based information about Soviet intentions to an American civilian and military population with woefully little understanding of the nature of the Communist threat.

His first surprise was his reception in Washington. He equated government with a cold and austere bureaucracy. The U.S. Army Intelligence officials greeted him respectfully, and professionally. They put him up at the Willard Hotel in downtown Washington, relatively lavish accommodations given Songa's frame of reference. After serving so many months in the menial labor pool, and after living his life in America under the shroud of suspicion, such a reception was particularly gratifying. He was back among military personnel, and despite the underlying mistrust that needed to be dispelled, Leon and the G2 officials displayed a mutual understanding and appreciation of each other's backgrounds.

On his first full day in Washington, he was met in the hotel and taken across the Potomac to the Pentagon to undergo his first formal interrogation. The deal he had brokered through the FBI, to stop the deportation order, was based on the assumption that he would prove to be useful as an informant. The Army needed to evaluate whether Leon was of any real value to them and whether his intelligence potential would be worth the effort necessary to take on the security risk. If he did not meet G2's requirements, the deal was off.

He passed his first series of evaluations resoundingly. He managed to impress a group of government bureaucrats who screen defectors from Communist countries all of the time—a jaded group, not easily excited by the targets of their interrogations.

Leon got them excited. His interrogators quickly understood that he was not like the other defectors. His disaffection for Communism seemed genuine. The positions he had held in the Polish Army, as a senior intelligence officer and military attaché, made him different from the others. His obvious intelligence, insight, and keen powers of observation set him apart. And not insignificantly, Leon was charming and likeable, and had acquired enough English at that point to be able to communicate some of his natural charm.

In Washington, D.C., 1950, the United States military had found a source who could provide them with detailed insights into the workings, the organization, the methods, strategies, capabilities, and the ethos of the then seemingly impenetrable Communist Polish and Soviet Armies. The information that Leon could provide was beyond anything otherwise available to the American intelligence community at that time, a time when human intelligence was still the primary source of information for the army. As relations with the Soviet-controlled region became increasingly strained, and the potential for war became a credible danger, Leon's knowledge was considered a prize beyond anything G2 could have hoped for. They badly wanted to tap his knowledge.

He was officially assigned to the Eurasian Division of G2's Intelligence Group, working simultaneously with the Polish and Russian desk. As an employee of the United States government, Leon would be paid fifty dollars a week. His job was, simply, to be debriefed.

Sometimes his days were filled with endless hours of one-on-one interviews, conducted in Polish or Russian, for the most part. At other times he was given intelligence information gathered through other sources, to verify, react to, or to interpret. Often, he was brought to a large briefing room, filled to capacity with key military personnel, to lecture and to answer questions, a translator by his side. Such was his appeal, that these lectures were always standing room only.

Leon was once again in an environment where he could shine. At the Pentagon, he found himself surrounded by intelligent, energetic, capable people, who had some understanding of what he had come from, and who respected, admired, and acknowledged his considerable accomplishments. On a personal level, it was a very positive time for the man who had had a very rough transition during his first year in America.

There was one glitch in the otherwise highly successful arrangement with the Pentagon—the security procedures. As was customary in these sensitive defector cases, Leon was given code names to protect his identity. Almost daily, he was assigned a new name and a string of security clearances tied to that name. But for Leon, whose understanding of English was still very rough, and his pronunciation even worse, the very American-sounding names assigned to him were more challenging than anyone had intended: Leon could never recognize or remember his name.

The problems with the security procedures were obvious from the start. On his first full day in Washington, the plan was set that FBI agents would meet him in the lobby of his hotel and escort him to the Pentagon. Through intricate communications, it had been relayed to him that his alias for this first day would be "Walter Smith." At the designated time, the undercover FBI agents arrived at the hotel, and asked the clerk to page Walter Smith.

The agents waited patiently in the lobby. There was no response. They asked the hotel clerk to repeat the page. Again, there was no response. Leon was sitting comfortably in a chair in the lobby, flipping through a newspaper, completely oblivious to the fact that the page was for him.

The FBI agents became more anxious, fearing that their defector had somehow duped them. Suddenly, Leon became aware of his error and the activity in the lobby. He realized that he was, in fact, Walter Smith. He presented himself to the agents and apologized.

G2 officials became used to the security mishaps. It happened again and again that Leon did not remember who he was supposed to be. Leon saw some humor in the situation. "Call me Chaim Yankel," he told them. "That I can remember." The G2 personnel saw less humor in a situation where highly classified military secrets were being shared between two enemy nations.

As well as things were going with the arrangements with the Army, the protection G2 afforded him did not assure Leon immunity from the INS bureaucrats. INS still viewed him as a defector whose plea for asylum had been rejected, and they considered his current status as temporary. They would not back off his case. Moreover, the FBI, with its own mandate as the counter-intelligence bureaucracy, was still monitoring Leon to potentially catch any suspicious activity that might suggest that he was acting as a double agent.

Ironically, in the wake of all this continued aggressive monitoring, the authorities at G2 grew to trust Leon remarkably quickly. But, as those who were more mistrustful of his motives were quick to point out, it was the Communist Polish authorities that had trusted him so explicitly, enough to grant his exit visa just one year earlier. So, should they trust him?

The competing agendas of the different Washington bureaucracies were fully transparent to Leon. He once again lived with that constant plaguing fear that at some point, someone in one of the agencies would put through the order to send him back to Poland—back to the jaws of death, as he thought of it. He knew from his own training in military intelligence, that out of necessity, his loyalty to the United States would always be in question. He would always feel the presence of someone whose sole job was to weed out individuals who posed a threat to national security.

Leon determined that the only way around this, the only way to rid himself of the constant fear of expulsion, was to start a fight—not just for legal residence in the United States, but also for citizenship. Citizenship would be the only guarantee of remaining in the country: the only guarantee of peace of mind, once and for all.

Nobody who worked with Leon ever doubted his loyalty to, and unqualified embracing of democratic ideals. They were all universally impressed with his skills as an assimilator. They believed this former Communist would make an impressive contribution to American society. But there was one person in the G-2 ranks that was particularly drawn to Leon's affability and sincerity, and would become his staunchest supporter in his quest for legal status in America. This individual, without exaggeration, would come to save Leon's life.

Her name was Dorothy Matlack, and when she spoke, people came to attention. She stood an impressive five-feet, nine-inches tall, but her stature was such that when she entered a room, she seemed to rise a full foot taller. She was the widow of an Army colonel who had been killed in the Philippines during the beginning of America's involvement in World War II, and she was so well connected that she counted the likes of General Dwight D. Eisenhower, and General Omar Bradley among her circle of close friends.

She was a brilliant, confident, big-hearted, and well-placed woman. And she liked and admired Leon Ajces from the moment she met him. Even though she was only about ten years his senior, he always respectfully referred to her as "Mrs. Matlack," never Dorothy. She never referred to him as anything other than "Major."

Her official function within G2 was a negotiator/expeditor for political asylum requests on behalf of the defectors they housed. Unofficially, she had become a powerful and trusted adviser to the Army Chief of Staff for Intelligence, giving her untold influence in the most upper and inside echelons of the United States government.

Government agencies worked very much in isolation, and Mrs. Matlack's job was to liaison with the INS on behalf of G2's highly valued defectors. INS had little appreciation for the value these people brought to the United States in terms of military intelligence, being more concerned with adhering to its rules and laws for residency and deportation, without regard to the need for exceptions to those rules. Mrs. Matlack worked to exercise those exceptions.

Mrs. Matlack and Leon had every business reason to like each other, but there was a personal bond that developed almost immediately. In Leon, Mrs. Matlack saw a wonderfully smart, insightful, charming, honest, future patriot. He would become her personal experiment. She would take this defector from the ideologically and economically impoverished Communist world, and let him see what he could accomplish in the riches of opportunity provided by a democracy. In Mrs. Matlack, Leon had an unparalleled advocate, who would exercise her considerable resources and connections, literally moving mountains if need be, to rescue him from his precarious immigration status. She would ensure that he could remain in this country.

Leon's appeal to Mrs. Matlack—as a potential *model* defector, the poster child for the democratic experiment, extended beyond her: it was widespread among all those who knew him at G2. Leon's colleagues at the Pentagon recognized something quite unusual in him as compared to the numerous other Eastern European defectors and informants with whom they had worked.

Most of the defectors from Communist regimes proved to be *basket cases*, in the words of a former G2 official, when it came to assimilating to America's capitalist society. They were completely ill equipped to function in an economy that rewarded an industrious and innovative approach. Most proved to be a liability to the country after they left the Pentagon, failing to maintain self-sufficiency once they left the protection of the government.

Everyone at G2 knew Leon's story would be different. They all saw in him an enthusiasm and a spark that they knew would drive him to success. Perhaps it was genetic, his mother's entrepreneurial spirit waiting to erupt inside him. Regardless of what drove him, as he recharged and retooled during the two years at the Pentagon, once again finding his self-respect and self-confidence, he soon felt more than ready to return to the civilian work force, and to act on his entrepreneurial instinct.

Leon was hungry to make his mark in the capitalist world, and G2 knew it was time to let him go. In 1952, through mutual agreement, Leon left the Pentagon, and returned to his life in New York City.

Leaving the Pentagon would bring a new set of challenges, and Leon knew full well that outside G2's protection he was vulnerable. He had now become a conspirator against his former country, and if the Polish government and Stalin's security forces were interested in expending the resources to hunt him down, he was certainly at risk. But the risk equation was difficult to calculate. He would never know how critically the Communists viewed his defection, or whether they might have predicted his collaboration with the United States Army. He knew people back in Poland would have suffered on his behalf. But realistically, how far did Stalin's reach extend?

Leon had proved he was a risk-taker. He would be appropriately cautious, but he refused to live his life on the run. As standard procedure, most G2 informants from the Communist countries changed their identities when they left G2. Leon would not. Leon Ajces was who he was, and he would live his life in the open, regardless of the potential consequences.

Mrs. Matlack would have to continue the fight with INS to allow him to stay in the country. Progress was made, and it soon advanced to a fight for citizenship, rather than a question of deportation; he received his green card shortly after leaving the Pentagon. He no longer faced the risk of deportation.

It was citizenship that was becoming increasingly important to Leon, as he invested more, and more of himself in living the American dream, divesting himself more, and more of his former life. He needed to be perceived as a fully legitimate, voting member of American society. He needed the protection of citizenship, both to reach closure on the deportation issue, as well as to regain control of his civil liberties. As a non-citizen, Leon had no recourse against the FBI, who continued to monitor his actions and tap his phone. Only as a citizen would he be entitled to all of the freedom and protection of an American. Mrs. Matlack knew and understood the significance of this; she made it her personal challenge to see that Leon Ajces would become a naturalized citizen of the United States.

11

From Comrade to Capitalist

Leon returned to work at the Novak News Company in 1952. They were only too happy to have him back. They understood little about his dealings with the Pentagon over the past two years; they were only relieved to know that his involvement with the FBI had nothing to do with the Mob ties to their business.

After two years in Washington, D.C., Leon returned to Novak, transformed. His English skills had measurably improved, and his confidence had been restored. He had been the *Major,* again, during his stint at the Pentagon, and was reconciled with his pre-defection identity. He had newfound purpose and clarity in his ambitions. He returned to Novak sensing that that the publishing distribution business would offer good opportunities for an ambitious, intelligent, tough, and logistically minded person.

The growth of the publishing distribution business in the New York metropolitan area had its share of intrigue. In many ways a gritty, dirty business—rife with corruption and Mafia-influenced Union workers—the distributors represented the underbelly of the otherwise glamorous world of magazine publishing.

Back in the 1920s, one company, the American News Company, ran a monopoly as the sole distributor of magazines and newspapers to newsstands and stores. As a monopoly, American News garnered so much power that eventually they started to have undue control over the publishers, to the point where they could tell them what to print in their magazines. The publishers, fearing this imbalance of power, took it upon themselves to break up the monopoly by financing individual truck drivers from American News to enable them to set up small, independent distribution businesses. In total, the publishers funded twenty-seven small businesses, providing monthly subsidies to the truck drivers, and carving out protected distribution territories for each to operate in.

Suddenly a number of uneducated truck drivers found themselves owners of small businesses, with a guaranteed stream of revenues. The *owners* had virtually no business training, and many of them were not particularly savvy, leaving the way for the few who had some innate business sense to seize a bigger piece of the business. Harry Novak was one of those with that business sense, and he began to widen his territory by merging with two other former drivers: Lester Scherin, and Harry Leibowitz.

This is the business landscape that Leon walked into as a non-English-speaking immigrant at Novak News: a quietly growing business, with guaranteed revenues, and tremendous opportunity, led by owners with little sophistication in the ways of operating a profitable business. And here was Leon Ajces, well-educated, possessing a strong business sense, highly trained in the most sophisticated military strategy, and with a deep understanding of the logistics of distribution. Only now, he would have to adapt that knowledge to the movement of millions of magazines and paperback books, instead of millions of soldiers and equipment during war. He sensed that, in time, he could make his mark in this business.

He was put back into the warehouse when he resumed his work at Novak, back on Sutton Street in Greenpoint, Brooklyn. Little had changed there, in the place where the FBI had arrived two years earlier, and made plans for his position with the Pentagon. Now, instead of simply sorting the magazines and books by their covers, he was promoted to the head of the book room. It was a monumental step down in prestige from his post at the Pentagon, but at least it was a few steps up from where he had left off. He now had several people working under him, and comfortably reassumed being in the position to bark orders at his underlings.

With little other diversion in his life at that time, Leon immersed himself in work. His understanding of the business was far wider than the narrow scope of his actual job, and his ambition compelled him to spend all of his spare time obsessively calculating ways in which the business could be more efficient. Certainly, nobody in the company asked him to do this, and nobody would have imagined that the "Russian guy," as they referred to him, with no wife or children, was working until three or four o'clock in the morning. There was no such work ethic in this business where a good, steady income was virtually guaranteed. In this Union-dominated environment, there was little call for ambition.

Typically, Leon would work at the office until the early evening; travel the one and one-half hours on the subway from Greenpoint, Brooklyn, to his home in the Bronx, and resume working at home, well into the night. He would sit at the one table in his small, dark, one-room apartment—a stark light bulb dangling over the table, a bottle of chilled vodka standing within reach. The five-and-dime-store stereo blasted grainy recordings of the Red Army Chorus, as he continued to calculate, analyze, plot, and strategize.

He acted as though he were the owner of Novak News. He worked as though the profits were going directly into his own pocket. He was compulsive and ambitious. And from all of this effort came the idea he had been looking for—the idea that would pull him from the warehouse, and put him in the front office.

It was the truck drivers' routing system that he had spent most of his time analyzing, drawing endless diagrams, following the driver from initial loading in the warehouse, through the deliveries to the newsstands and magazine shops, and back to the warehouse at the end of the day. Applying his years of military training, and the deployment of troops and equipment across hundreds of miles as his context, Leon recalculated the process by which the truck drivers ran their routes. He recognized certain basic inefficiencies in the process, that when eliminated, would result in tremendous savings in terms of time, effort, gasoline, and all of the associated costs.

His plan would require a total overhaul of the current complex Byzantine routing system (in the pre-computer age), and a major investment of time and retraining. Consequently, Leon would need to sell his idea to the owners of Novak, directly. Leon recognized his English skills would not allow him to persuasively present such a sophisticated proposal to the *big bosses*, thus, he enlisted his cousin Rose, as he had done before, to step in as his translator.

The owners agreed to listen to what he had to say. When Leon walked into their offices, armed with intricate drawings and diagrams, they were taken aback by the amount of work he had done. When he was finished presenting, Leon smiled. He saw the disbelief on Harry Leibowitz and Lester Scherin's faces. All Lester could say was "how did this Russian with the bad English from the book room come up with this?" "This is amazing," Harry responded. "Can you really make this happen?" he asked Leon, skeptically. Leon nodded.

Within days, Leon was catapulted from the warehouse to the office, and given the task of overseeing the implementation of the new routing system. It proved to be hugely successful. Within two years, he was made General Manager, in charge of all daily operations, of what was by then, through continuing acquisitions and growth, known as Imperial News Company. Leon was on his way, and was loving every minute of it.

12

And Along Came Betty

With his increasing responsibility, and his obsessive commitment to his work, there was little Leon did outside of the Imperial News Company. By 1956, he still kept mostly to himself, and saved what little socializing he did for his family, who was more determined than ever to find their cousin a wife. He had his green card. He had a good job, with a decent salary. Everyone agreed; it was time for him to settle down.

Still conscious of his poor English, he preferred to keep his distance from people outside the family, for both the language reasons, as well as people's misconceptions about the Communist association. But Leon's increasing professional success made him significantly more confident, socially. And with that confidence, he was able to realize that what he had considered to be a terrible liability—his accent and his *foreign ways*—could actually be used to his advantage. Many women, he discovered, were attracted to his exotic and charming European ways.

Now that he had some money in his pocket, he was able to discover the Jewish dating Mecca up in the Catskill Mountains, the now fabled resort community located about two hours from New York City. Mostly he stayed at the famous Grossinger's Hotel. He would go alone, with just a change of clothes, and his mandolin in hand. He had a single purpose to his trips, and executed his plans to ensure that purpose was met.

Leon would carefully orchestrate his moves at the hotel, choosing to perch himself in public spaces—either in the grand hotel lobby, or on the sprawling, well-manicured lawn. He positioned himself perfectly to look wistful, and soulful, as he served up the lyrical melodies on his mandolin, an elixir to the eligible young Jewish women roaming the grounds of the resort. He was highly successful in his seduction scheme. But much to the disappointment of his overly involved and marriage-minded family, none of these mountain affairs were intended to amount to anything more than a weekend of Borscht belt passion.

Back home, work was starting to make some new demands on Leon's social life. The magazine publishing business was very social, and relationships were formed through the requisite networking and cavorting at the innumerable events that played out during the course of the year. In the past, Leon would flee from these kinds of events, as shy and intensely private, as he was. Loud, crowded cocktail parties, with fast-talking people, were still challenging for Leon's improving, but limited English. Once, when a leggy blonde brushed by him at one of these events, she whispered, "hi ya', cutie pie," in his ear. He didn't understand her flirtation to be an invitation to further conversation. He spent the next few minutes trying to sort through the possible flavor of *cutie* pie. He knew cherry pie, and blueberry pie, but had never come across *cutie* pie.

As he rose in the company, however, he realized that he had no choice but to participate in the publishers' social events, if he wanted to truly make it big in the business. Besides, the payoff for attendance at these affairs was the liberal flow of alcohol. And, of course, Leon loved to drink.

◆   ◆   ◆

He first laid eyes on Betty Green at a party in October 1956. The party was in a *swank* Manhattan restaurant, hosted by Select Magazines. Betty was not in the publishing business, nor did she drink. She was there with a friend, who had convinced her to go; it wasn't her scene, and after only a few minutes she was ready to leave.

Leon noticed Betty in the well-dressed crowd. He liked the way she looked, and decided to make his move. He had done this so many times before; he never would have imagined that this time would be his last.

They talked for a bit, the usual small talk. Betty was amused and entertained by this man who was clearly different from anyone she had ever met before, so when he asked for her phone number, she complied. She left the party, not giving too much thought to the handsome stranger with the heavy Russian accent, and the charming manners.

Betty Green was twenty-seven-years-old, and had already had her own share of life experience. At the time, most twenty-seven-year-old Jewish women, from middle-class families in Jackson Heights, Queens were married, and home taking care of their children. Betty had chosen a very different path.

By 1956, she had already retired from nine years of touring as a jazz musician, on the road, as part of an *all-girl* group. She had seen the inside of every nightclub, in every little town in America, as a stand-up bass player, going out on her own into the rough and tumble, three o'clock-in-the-morning-world of jazz music. And while her mother, Hanna, was aghast at her daughter's chosen profession, she acknowledged that music was in her daughter's soul. Betty's father, Louis Green, who had died suddenly when Betty was only fifteen, had also been a professional musician, playing clarinet in the famous NBC Orchestra, under the leadership of Maestro Arturo Toscanini. Louis was, coincidentally, a Russian Jewish immigrant from Byelorussia, having immigrated to America as a child in the early 1900s. Hanna Green had lived through life with a musician, and she knew her daughter had been possessed by the musical spell.

Betty was an extremely talented, very serious musician. A classically trained pianist, she turned her attention to the double bass at the prestigious High School of Music and Art in Manhattan, graduating in 1947. Just after graduation, at the impressionable age of seventeen, she left home and hit the road with her jazz band. By 1953, Betty's group was a winning act on television's *Arthur Godfrey Show*.

By the time Leon met Betty that evening in October 1956, she had logged thousands of miles hauling her double bass through countless smoky bars, and even more groping drunk men—men who were more intrigued with the gender of her jazz group, than with the music they played. She was weary of the club life, and had recently returned home to New York City to pursue a career in the theater. She had fought against mainstream society's expectations for the kind of life a young woman in America in the 1950s was supposed to be living. But now, despite her fiery independence, Betty was starting to believe that it might be time to settle down and get married.

Leon called her a few weeks after they met at the party. Betty hadn't given him much thought, otherwise occupied with another boyfriend at the time. The man she was dating was not Jewish—a big disappointment to her mother—and when Leon called, she agreed to see him again. He came to her house in Jackson Heights, a locale he knew too well. Amazingly, Betty lived only blocks from Leon's cousin, Clara—only blocks from the house where he had first lived upon arriving in America. It was an uncanny coincidence.

He took Betty to lunch at a local Italian restaurant, in Jackson Heights, and then brought her to Clara's house. His family was only too happy to meet the nice Jewish girl who lived only blocks away. They fussed over Betty to the point where Leon quickly became uncomfortable. They left shortly, and said their goodbyes to each other.

The sparks did not fly during their first date, but Betty continued to find Leon charming, handsome, and completely unlike anyone she had ever dated. Leon captivated her with his stories of his past, and Betty talked of her life as a musician. A mutual interest was clearly forming.

She did not hear from Leon for several weeks. Then, one Monday night, he called again. Imperial News had purchased a table at a cancer benefit, and Leon was expected to attend with a date. The benefit was only a few days away—that Friday night—and Leon asked Betty to join him. He did not apologize for the short notice.

In the throes of her acting pursuits, Betty was to perform that Friday night in a production put on by the studio where she was studying. She told him she was sorry, but she could not go. Leon had little appreciation for her acting aspirations. He hung up the phone, furious. "This one's a 'priza'…a princess," he thought to himself. "She thinks she's some big actress. Forget her!"

But two days later, he called her again. He openly admitted that he had tried every available woman he knew, but he simply couldn't find a date for the benefit. He told her his bosses were insisting that he not come alone. Betty was becoming put off by his overbearing insistence, and was about to tell him "no," firmly, when he threw her a little more incentive. Leon told her Harry Belafonte would be the featured performer at the benefit.

In America, in 1956, Betty was among the millions of women who thought Harry Belafonte, and his smooth silver-tongued voice, was nothing short of a divine gift. She thought for a moment. She weighed the chance to see Harry Belafonte live, in an intimate setting, against her acting career. There would be other roles. Belafonte won, hands down. "OK, I'll go with you," she told Leon. He was delighted.

The benefit was in Brooklyn, at the Town and Country Nightclub on Flatbush Avenue. Since Leon lived in one end of New York City, up in the Bronx, and Betty lived in the other end of New York City, in Queens, she told him she would just drive herself there, and meet him at the club.

Betty arrived at the club and found her date. Leon greeted her warmly, took her to the table, and briefly introduced her to all of his colleagues. "This won't be too bad," she tried to reassure herself, even though she did not know a soul other than Leon. It was a loud, boisterous, drinking crowd. Betty did not drink. Leon loved to drink.

Within minutes after greeting her, Leon told Betty he needed to talk business with several men from the industry who were also at the party.

Before she had the chance to answer, he disappeared, leaving her sitting alone at the long banquet table.

She made some polite small talk. Then she spoke to no one. And no one spoke to her. Time passed, and Leon was still nowhere to be seen. Eventually, dinner was served. Betty was still alone, and ate her meal in silence. She watched the crowd get drunker and drunker, and became angrier and angrier that she had allowed Leon to coerce her into giving up her plans, only to be completely abandoned and ignored by her date.

Harry Belafonte performed, and she watched the performance alone. After the show, Betty hastily packed up her things to leave. It was then that Leon emerged, swaggering back to the table, completely and utterly inebriated.

He fell all over Betty, and started to plead, in his drunken slur, "Did ya' miss me baby?"

"Get away from me," Betty snapped back.

"Hey baby, where are you going? Come home with me tonight," he mumbled.

At that moment, Harry Belafonte walked by their table. He needed to squeeze through a small area to go up a staircase leading to the stage, where Barry Gray, a venerable DJ of the time, was doing a live radio broadcast.

Leon noticed the entertainer behind him, and decided to show his approval with an affectionate slap on the shoulder—a slap packed with such ferocity, that the drunken Leon lost his balance and fell into Belafonte. Belafonte was caught off guard, and stumbled off the staircase, onto the floor.

Betty watched in horror as this scene unfolded inches away from her. Everyone rushed to assist Belafonte. Betty looked at Leon, and plotted her immediate escape from this crazy, drunken Russian. She had made some dating mistakes before, but this one would take the prize.

She had just stood up to get her coat, when her date's cousin, Leon Berkule, also attending the party, rushed up to her. It was almost 3:00 AM.

"Hey, we're all going to Coney Island to get hot dogs at Nathan's," Berkule told her.

"No, thank you, I'm going home," Betty responded curtly.

"I'm not asking you to come," Berkule said. "I need someone to drive Leon home. He's too drunk to come out with us, and I don't think he should take the subway in his condition."

Betty had been abandoned, molested, and witness to Leon's *assault* of Harry Belafonte. She looked at Berkule in disbelief. "Drive him home!" Betty thought. "Are you kidding?"

She lived in Queens. He lived up in the Bronx. And they were in Brooklyn. Even if she wanted to spend another minute with this man, and she did not, she would not have wanted to navigate her way through the unfamiliar streets of the Bronx. Berkule continued to wait for her answer. Betty looked at Leon, now slumped over in a chair. "God help me," she said. "Follow me to the car."

Leon Berkule and several of the Imperial News co-workers managed to pour Leon into the passenger seat of Betty's car. She looked over at her *date* and started to drive off.

"Where do you live?" she asked him. Leon mumbled back incoherently.

"WHERE DO YOU LIVE?" she screamed this time.

He again mumbled, but this time she could understand the address. She knew he lived somewhere near the Grand Concourse, a main thoroughfare. She figured if she could just get that far, they would manage to find his house.

"Tell me how to get there!" she demanded of him.

But this time, there was no answer. He had passed out in the seat, and was snoring loudly.

The stench of liquor in the car was unbearable, particularly for Betty, the non-drinker. On that late October night, at 4:00 in the morning, despite the chill in the air, she rolled all of the windows down to avoid getting sick herself, and sped aimlessly through the deserted streets of New York City. After more than one hour of driving, and three stops for directions, she managed to find his apartment building—54 Featherbed Lane. It was almost 5:30 in the morning by the time she pulled up in front of his house. She opened the passenger door.

"GET OUT!" she screamed in his ear. He awoke just enough to stumble out the door, onto the sidewalk. When he realized he was home, he started to scream at her.

"Why did you take me home?" he said accusingly. "You should have put me on the subway," he continued to rave in his slurred and accented speech.

She looked at him for a moment, and considered whether she should help him into the apartment building. In disgust, she made up her mind, slammed the car door shut, and drove off. The car continued to reek of stale liquor for days, a lingering reminder of an evening she hoped to forget.

It took a whole week for Leon to call and apologize for his behavior. While her instincts told her to hang up, he was once again that charming and well-mannered man that she had met the first time. He seemed so genuinely sorry, and so intent on seeing her to make it up to her, that she actually, against her better judgment, agreed to go out with him again.

He was an enormously attractive, intelligent, commanding, powerful, and more than slightly, mysterious man. Betty figured she had lived through the worst with him. What did she have to lose? They began dating regularly. His retreats to the Catskills in pursuit of women ended. Betty broke up with the boyfriend she had been dating.

It was her first visit to his apartment that led Betty to understand just how different their worlds were. It was a prelude to the adjustments she would have to make to be with this man. Up until this point, she had seen only the outside of 54 Featherbed Lane in the

Bronx, at 5:30 in the morning, when she delivered the drunk Leon to the sidewalk, before speeding off. But now, Betty would see the inside of the apartment, and see how this man who was capturing her heart, lived.

She entered the dark, dingy, one-room apartment. A few scattered pieces of unmatched furniture barely filled the space. "You want something to drink?" Leon asked, pointing toward the small refrigerator. "I just need to finish up something I am working on." Betty nodded and helped herself.

She opened his refrigerator. It was empty, except for the rows of bottles of chilled vodka. She continued to survey her surroundings. "Where the hell am I?" Betty thought to herself. The meager possessions told the story of his favorite haunts. The few forks and spoons lying on the counter were all stamped with the label "Automat," *borrowed* from the famous self-service restaurant in Manhattan. The bathroom towels all read "Grossingers," lifted from the famous Catskill resort that served as the site for Leon's weekend trysts. The Formica kitchen table was covered with handwritten telephone numbers, written, with ink, directly onto the table.

When Betty saw her own name and telephone number on the list, she realized the table was serving double duty as Leon's *little black book* of the women he dated. She turned and peered through his record collection, and saw mostly Red Army Chorus recordings, and Russian folk music. Certainly, this relationship was going to offer its share of challenges.

Differences aside, just five months later, Leon approached Hanna Green, and asked for her daughter's hand in marriage. The man from the shtetl met with his future mother-in-law and laid out his prospects. Above all, he pledged to always take care of her daughter. Hanna was impressed with his sincerity, and old-fashioned formality.

On October 20, 1957, scarcely a year after the fiasco at the Town and Country nightclub, they stood together at the Park Royal Hotel, on Central Park West, and became husband and wife. By 5:00 PM, the bartender for the reception announced they had run out of liquor. Betty maneuvered her drunken husband, who had consumed much of the alcohol supply for the wedding reception, into the car and drove off to a honeymoon suite at the Concord Hotel in the Catskills.

By breakfast the next morning, the first full day of their married life, Betty was delirious with fever. By Tuesday afternoon, the second day of their married life, Betty managed to drive the two hours home through her Asian flu-induced delirium, park the car in the Bronx, and crawl to her new home—an apartment one flight up from Leon's bachelor apartment. Betty slept for the next six days. When she finally woke up, she was ready to start her life as Mrs. Leon Ajces.

◆　　　◆　　　◆

Marriage was an adjustment for both of them. He was strong and opinionated, and used to being alone. He operated his home life with the same order and precision as he had his military life. Leon was a perfectionist, who had been trained to view the world in black and white; there was little gray, and little room for compromise.

Betty and Leon wanted to start a family right away. She was twenty-seven, already considered to be on the older side for a first-time mother. He was an impossibly old, forty-one. And for all of his rough exterior and scarring experiences, he loved babies and children, and had only the warmest of memories of his own childhood as part of large, loving family.

But nature was unkind to the newlyweds, as Betty suffered through a series of miscarriages. After many procedures and countless tests, it was determined that Betty could not successfully carry a baby to full-term. If they were committed to having children, adoption would be their only alternative.

They agreed to explore adoption possibilities, and hired a lawyer to begin the process. Because of Leon's age, and his background, he convinced Betty that the mainstream adoption channels, working through an American agency, would be unavailable to them. "Nobody is going to place a child in a family where the father is a defector from a Communist country," he argued. "If you want to do this, we need to do this another way." Betty agreed.

They worked through the lawyer. Before long, the lawyer contacted them with good news. He had identified a possible adoption opportunity in Greece.

Betty was beside herself with excitement as they made preparations to travel to Greece for the required initial meeting. After all of the disappointments she had suffered with each failed pregnancy, she allowed herself to become more hopeful that they might actually realize the dream of having a family. The process had been particularly hard on Betty. Even though Leon had never placed blame on her, she silently harbored the guilt that it had been her deficiency that kept them from having children. Now she saw a light at the end of the tunnel.

Two weeks before they were to depart for Greece, Leon changed his mind. "I don't think that this is a good idea," he told her one night as she was planning for the trip. For months he stood by her side through the planning and investigation of possible adoption opportunities. Now, suddenly, he was telling her he couldn't go through with it.

Betty was blindsided by the turnaround. "What are you saying?" she demanded of him. "How can you suddenly change your mind about something this big?" He told her it had everything to do with his past. What would happen when the Greek officials started investigating him? What if they contacted the Polish government to learn more? How could they take the risk? Betty was devastated by her husband's words. But even more devastating was her realization that trying to reason with him would be futile. She knew her husband well enough, by now. Leon had made up his mind. Compromise was not in his universe.

Days later, after the initial shock had worn off, Betty pressed him further. "Is this really all about your past?" she asked. He looked at her, his eyes fixing intently on hers. "I don't want it, if it's not mine. I can't be the father, if it doesn't come from me." Betty's eyes filled with tears. "I'm sorry, but you have to make your choice, Betty," he said gently but matter-of-factly. "Children, or me." Betty chose her husband, and resigned herself to a life without children.

13

An American Citizen

Almost ten years had passed from the time Leon had made his initial petition to become a citizen of the United States. Even with Dorothy Matlack continuing to work tirelessly on his case, pulling every formidable string she had to pull, the process still dragged on.

Time-after-time, Leon would subject himself to the endless and seemingly pointless INS interviews, in which they would ask the same questions over-and-over again. "Are you a Communist?" "Were you ever a member of the Communist Party?" "Why do you say you were born in Russia when your birth certificate claims you were born in Poland?"

The suspicious questioning coming from the bureaucratic *talking head*, following a script, with no understanding of world history, infuriated Leon to no end. "*Shmucks*, all of them." He was not satisfied with his green card. He wanted to become an American citizen. He wanted to vote, and to be a part of the American democratic system. He wanted his civil liberties. This was more important to him than anything else, so much so, that after he and Betty got engaged, he warned her that if he did not get his citizenship in the next cycle of application reviews, he would seriously consider moving to Israel.

Leon had an INS appointment scheduled in 1961, and threatened that it would be his last, regardless of the outcome. Mrs. Matlack insisted on making the trip to New York, to personally accompany the *Major*, at the interview.

When they sat down in the interview room at the INS office, the usual questioning began. As the interviewer immediately began to rehash the same questions of nationality, and Leon's political allegiances, that had repeatedly come up in prior interviews, Mrs. Matlack slammed her hand on the table. "This is an outrage," she declared and proceeded to stand up and storm out of the room.

She walked briskly to a pay phone located just outside the interview room, and made a phone call to a senior Justice Department official in Washington. She demanded that Leon be cleared for citizenship, on the spot, then and there. She would not hang up the phone until the order had been put through. And just for added emphasis, she suggested that the interviewer, whom she considered grossly incompetent, be fired.

Several months later, Mrs. Matlack called to tell them Leon's citizenship papers were on the way. She wanted to come to New York City to personally celebrate their victory.

Betty and Leon met her at a restaurant in Greenwich Village to mark the occasion. At dinner, Mrs. Matlack leaned over and whispered to Betty, "You know, your signature is required on the paperwork for it to be official. I would hold out for a mink coat before you agree to sign anything." Betty laughed. She signed the papers. The mink coat came, many years later.

He was naturalized by the United State District Court, Eastern District, Brooklyn, on February 27, 1962. Before they went for the swearing-in ceremony, Betty and Leon discussed changing their last name on the papers. AJCES was a ridiculously difficult name for English speakers to pronounce or spell. If they just dropped the *j*, they would make their lives easier by changing the name to Aces. However, in the course of the commotion of the swearing in, the clerk went ahead and recorded the name of the new citizen of the United States, Leon Ajces, just as it read on the papers.

Betty and Leon looked at each other and understood that Leon Ajces, the American, would bear the same family name, and be the same man, as Lazar Ajces of the Russian empire, the Polish citizen, and the Soviet citizen. Only now, as an American, he would be able to laugh, love, live, and achieve without fear. For the decorated war hero, and the enormously successful businessman, this day, without question, was the day he realized his proudest accomplishment.

Mrs. Matlack, and the G-2 officials proclaimed that their *experiment* had proven resoundingly successful. Leon was *their* defector, and had become their personal proof of the promise of the American experience. The pillars of democracy and freedom carried this defector from poverty and oppression, to the heights of entrepreneurial success, and Mrs. Matlack and the others derived enormous personal pride from Leon's mastery of the American capitalist system.

In the 1970s, after Leon's successes as a businessman had become readily apparent, a dinner was held by G-2, in Leon's honor, at the Georgetown Hotel in Washington, D.C. Even though almost twenty years had elapsed, many of his colleagues from the Pentagon were in attendance. Mrs. Matlack was one of the speakers at the dinner. In her remarks she related that out of all the defectors and political refugees she helped throughout her career, Leon was by far her favorite. Never, she added, had she seen someone give so much to this country, and ask for so little in return. Leon even chose to forgo the nominal government pension he was entitled to after his tenure with the Army intelligence group. The only thing he demanded in return for his efforts was to be a fully participating member of American society.

14

Owning Imperial

On Palm Sunday, 1960, Lester Scherin, one of the two remaining owners of Imperial News Company, dropped dead from a heart attack. Leon was at home when he got the call. It was the first time Betty had seen her husband cry.

When the shock and grief passed, Leon turned his attention to more pragmatic concerns: the consideration of the longer-term issues of the business. With Lester gone, Harry Leibowitz was now the sole partner and owner. Leon knew Harry could not run the company alone. Leon, who by now was the General Manager, also knew that his own efforts had contributed immeasurably to the success and growth of the company over the past several years, and felt it was time to be compensated commensurately. Leon wanted an equity stake in the company.

Harry had a son, David, who was working for the company, and was presumably heir apparent. To date, David had been relegated to the warehouse as opposed to the front office, becoming a Union member, and working with the drivers. David's own mother had expressed her doubts to her husband whether her son had the *stuff* necessary to run the business. But just before Lester's death, Harry had asked Leon to begin breaking David into the office—he knew Leon would have to be the one to teach his son how to run the business. Leon agreed, seeing a future where he would be given a share of the business, and eventually become partners with David, after Harry retired. A third potential partner emerged as well—Lenny Manza—who ran the floor, and the Unions. Lenny was a key player in the smooth operations of the underside of Imperial News Company. He had the necessary Mob relationships to ensure that the truck drivers, part of the Mafia-controlled Mail Deliverers Union, did what was needed, and stayed out of trouble.

In the early 1960s, Harry offered to sell Leon and Lenny ten percent each of the business, for a nominal sum. Leon was satisfied. It was a start. But after making the offer, Harry made a mistake that almost cost him the future success of his business: he changed his mind.

Harry got nervous about giving outsiders a piece of the business, and decided he wanted to keep it all for David. Leon was a man who worked on trust and loyalty. To betray his loyalty was the most egregious assault one could make against Leon Ajces. Leon had spent a lifetime determining whom he could trust, and whom he considered loyal; many times his life depended on it. His benchmark for the consequences of betrayal was significantly higher than most.

If Leon trusted you, you were in. If he didn't trust you, you might as well have not existed in his eyes. And if you betrayed his trust, you had better be prepared for the response. Leon didn't posture. He acted on his instincts. Harry was unfortunate enough to have tested Leon's boundaries of trust, and he grossly misjudged the reaction he would elicit by cutting Leon out of the picture.

Days after Harry recanted his offer of ownership, Leon turned around and gave two-weeks notice. He was ready to walk away. He was not bluffing. He knew his worth to the company, he knew his skills in building a successful business, and he was prepared to leave Imperial and buy his own agency in Pennsylvania. In only a few days, he had lined up the investors, and had identified an agency to buy.

Harry knew that Imperial's success was dependent on Leon. Harry wasn't prepared to give up the future growth of the extremely profitable business over a ten percent share. After Leon's maelstrom of a response, Harry changed his mind, again; Leon got his share. But the relationship between the aging Harry, and the vigorous and confident Leon, would forever be diminished. Over time, Harry participated less, and less, in the daily operations of the business, and Leon, along with David and Lenny Manza, was running the company.

By the late 1960s, the partners had carved out their areas of responsibility, and the business hummed along successfully. Leon was in charge of all internal operations—the organization and management of the business. David was in charge of the external operations, building the relationships, and handling the entertaining and the networking with the publishers—the necessary social side of the business that the more introverted and private Leon detested. Lenny handled the drivers, and the Union, and was kept at arms length.

Leon was meticulous and organized, and ran the company the way he ran his military operation. There was no tolerance for inefficiency, poor performance, or mistakes, and while he was never known to raise his voice, he managed his people as he had once been managed in the army—through an air of quiet, pervasive fear. "When they walk by me, they have full pants," Leon would sometimes say with a sense of satisfaction, as he talked about the employees milling about the Imperial plant. As a result, he had his share of enemies, those who resented his unforgiving and strict disciplinarian approach. But even those who disliked him acknowledged that his ability to squeeze out the waste, and cut costs by improving efficiency, is what made Imperial far more successful than its competitors.

As demanding and exacting as he was, he was also universally recognized to be generous, and fair to his employees. He had a particular soft spot for the immigrants who showed up at his door, looking for work. It had not been too long ago that he was standing in their spot, with limited English, and desperate for work, judged by simpleminded employers to be unfit for even the most low-level jobs. He never forgot those early days in America, and went out of his way to give jobs—even create jobs if necessary—to immigrants, particularly Russian and Polish immigrants.

One day, an Irishman, named Vinny Doyle, came in to interview with Leon. With a wife and many children to support, he was looking for any job at all, as long as it paid an honest salary. Leon noticed Vinny seemed unusually anxious during the interview. "What are you running from?" he asked the Irishman, bluntly. "I killed someone," Vinny replied. "Long ago." Leon hired him on the spot. He admired Vinny's honesty, and knew he could be trusted.

By 1971, Lenny became ill, and David and Leon bought out his share of the business. Now it was just the two of them, and they grew to become a highly effective team, playing to each other's strengths. They developed a good cop/bad cop routine in negotiations and business dealings.

David had to take on the interface with the Union now that Lenny was gone. Leon would have nothing to do with the Union, even though the business was completely dependent on successful negotiation and ongoing maintenance of the relationship. Leon made no secret of his hatred for the Union, and the Mafia influence in their business. He hated the corruption, the theft, and the fact that in the 1970s, these uneducated Union truck drivers cleared more than $60,000 in salary. He called them thieves.

The Union had managed to negotiate contracts that guaranteed at least three hours of overtime pay per day, for the drivers—regardless of actual hours worked. The contracts also protected drivers from being fired for stealing even if they were caught, as they frequently were, pilfering cash or merchandise. If a newsstand complained about a particular driver, that newsstand might not receive magazine deliveries for several days.

The whole proposition disgusted Leon, and he was famous for putting forth his version of diplomacy for Union negotiations: in lieu of taking the time to negotiate with the Union leaders, he suggested they should just "put them up against a wall and shoot them." Some publishers viewed Leon's undisguised hatred for the Union as truly courageous; others viewed it as careless, given the extent of power held by the Union party leaders. The Union had the potential to derail the business through job walkouts and other tactics, including the very real possibility of causing physical harm.

Leon didn't care. He was not intimidated. He had lived through Hitler. He had survived Stalin. These small-time Mob thugs paled in comparison.

◆   ◆   ◆

Despite the inconvenience of the Mafia influence, Imperial News Company continued to grow at an astronomical pace. The money was starting to flow into Leon's wallet. Leon and Betty, who had *tightened the belt* to leave the Bronx—Betty forgoing an engagement ring, so they could put a down payment on their first home on Long Island, just after they married—were now able to move again.

This time they bought a house in the affluent community of Old Westbury, complete with swimming pool and two wooded acres of land. The cash coming in allowed them to build additions to their homes, take cruises, and buy second homes in Florida.

Leon was quickly becoming a wealthy American, yet, his day-to-day lifestyle, outside the houses they owned, revealed nothing of his new-found wealth. Already almost sixty years old, Leon did not know how to live differently. He did not know how to *be* rich, nor did he have any interest in adopting new attitudes or lifestyles.

He continued to work twelve-to-fourteen-hour days. Other than attending publishing-related social functions, Betty and Leon mostly stayed home, socializing primarily with family and a growing contingent of newly arrived Russian emigrants.

By 1977, the boy from the shtetl entered the pantheon of American capitalists: he became a millionaire.

The 1970s were the heady years for the enormously successful Imperial News Company, and their reputation as the most honest and trustworthy of all the distributors in this otherwise corrupt business, allowed them to take risks that others could not. The big coup that catapulted Leon into a new stratosphere of financial success came through a daring acquisition in 1971. At that time, the company expanded outside the metropolitan New York area, and branched into the publishing distribution market in Puerto Rico. Leon and David had purchased a much sought-after, under-performing agency—sight unseen—for the sum of $825,000. Leon recognized the enormous potential of this horribly mismanaged agency, and the as yet, unrealized potential for the distribution of Spanish language magazines and paperback books.

He spent eight months living in Puerto Rico, working sixteen-hour days. During that time, Leon turned the Puerto Rico operation into a profitable, smoothly running business. He also fell in love with Puerto Rico. He loved the Caribbean climate and culture. He loved the parties, and the entertaining he and Betty did in their lavish apartment, overlooking the blue-green Caribbean waters, in the upscale Condado area, in an apartment rented from the niece of the governor of Puerto Rico. And most of all, he loved his workforce of young Puerto Rican women, all of whom were attractive, hard working, and shamelessly loyal to their beloved patron, *Señor* Leon.

He was in his element, and happier than he had ever been at any time in his adult life. But eventually, the travel demands of shuttling back and forth from New York to San Juan became too much. It was time to move on. Leon and David made the decision to sell the Puerto Rico interest, only four years later. But in those four short years, Leon had managed to turn around a tidy profit of more than two million dollars through the sale of the business.

Puerto Rico may have been gone, but Leon continued to find ways to mix business and pleasure. The 1970s saw the explosive growth of a new genre of magazine. New magazines meant more volume for distribution; more volume meant more money for Imperial News Company.

The sexual revolution of the late 1960s had spawned the liberation of the pornography business, and the birth of a broad market for porn magazines brought Leon into the forefront. His company would get the magazines into the hands of eager readers. As a key partner in the distribution of these new magazines, he gained entrance into the infamously hedonistic worlds of the equally infamous publishers.

Leon now found himself a key-carrying member of the Playboy Club, and obliged to attend meetings at such salacious places as Manhattan's upscale sex palace, Plato's Retreat. Bob Guccione, publisher of *Penthouse Magazine*, was particularly fond of Leon, and used him as an adviser, requiring Leon to frequently meet with Guccione at his fabled brownstone mansion, on Manhattan's Upper Eastside.

It was at the Guccione homestead that Leon, continuously surrounded by scantily clad Penthouse models, lounging by the expansive indoor pool, found it hardest to concentrate on business. "Someone is smiling down on me," he would think to himself, as he sank into the overstuffed couches, and watched the parade of models. Leon, the man who at sixty looked easily ten years younger, the man who still had a libido running on overdrive, the man who during the war made his way through women from Poland to Berlin, now felt sure he would have a heart attack on the spot from the intensity of his temptation-induced palpitations.

15

Staring Down the Mafia

By 1978, Leon could no longer ignore the Mafia presence in his business. It came face-to-face with him, everyday, in the form of a deceptively benign, diminutive, aging Jewish man, named Irving Bitz.

Irving Bitz had the official title of "Labor Negotiator," for Imperial News Company, a euphemism for his real role as Mob *placater*. Bitz was a colorful character, with a lifetime of Mafia connections and underworld dealings. The most colorful spot on his resume was his role as a young *thug* negotiator on behalf of the Mob, in the famous Lindbergh baby kidnapping.

If Leon had his way, Bitz would have disappeared from his business, and his life. Bitz decided to reciprocate Leon's very public dislike for him by keeping him within arms length at all times. Irving Bitz made it his business to know exactly where Leon was, every minute of the day. Wherever Leon went, Irving followed.

At 6:30 in the morning, Leon would walk into his driveway, ready to leave for work. Irving would be there, parked, motor running, his bald head peering over the steering wheel of his Cadillac Sedan de Ville. "Come on in, I'll take you to work," Irving would coax, morning-after-morning. Irving knew Leon did not drive. He knew Betty always drove her husband to work. Leon always ignored the offer, climbing into the passenger seat next to Betty. "What is he doing here?" Betty asked. "Never mind, just drive," Leon answered. Irving would trail along behind them.

Irving often informed Leon that he would accompany him to important meetings with the publishers in Manhattan. Leon certainly didn't like it, but he accepted the intrusion, understanding that his protest was not worth the effort. "Just keep your mouth shut during the meeting," Leon would warn. On one occasion, as they finished the meeting, and walked down Sixth Avenue, the aging Irving attempted to flex his Mafia muscles. Irving stopped walking and pointed to a building across the street from where they stood. "See that window," Irving told Leon. "That's the exact office where I used to hang out with Legs Diamond." Leon wasn't impressed. He had no idea who Legs Diamond was.

There was no way for Leon to get rid of him. Early in the rise of the publishing distribution business, Bitz had served as the central intermediary with the Mob for all of the small distribution agencies, making the necessary payoffs to avoid strikes, walkouts, violence, and the host of other unpleasant incidents that might otherwise have occurred at the workplace. When the FBI began investigating the Mob influence in the business, Irving took the rap for all of the agency heads, taking the blame for the payoffs to the Mafia, rather than naming the people on whose behalf he was making the payoffs. When he was released from prison, no distribution agency wanted anything to do with him, knowing he was a magnet for continued FBI scrutiny.

But Harry Leibowitz had promised Irving a job in exchange for protecting him, and Harry made good on the promise. When he was released from prison, Irving became a full-time employee of Imperial. Now, Leon, a man who appreciated loyalty, considered himself beholden to Harry's promise. The difference was, that under *Harry's* watch, the Mob was considered a necessary nuisance in the business. Under *Leon's* watch, the Mob was not considered necessary. Leon was prepared to stand up to what he considered to be criminals, pilfering from the company's profits. He wanted the Union to be Mob-free, and he was not intimidated by their threats.

◆   ◆   ◆

On a hot July day in 1978, Leon was unknowingly liberated from Irving's shadowy presence. Irving was not in his driveway that morning. In the mid-morning, a call came into the executive office at Imperial News Company. David took the call. "We have Irving Bitz," the caller claimed. "Follow these directions if you want him back alive."

The kidnapper demanded a ransom of $150,000 in cash. David informed Leon of the situation, and Leon looked at him blankly. "You want to pay it, don't you?" Leon asked. David shrugged, and nodded. "What else can we do?" Leon paused. David was the one who had to deal with the Unions. He would have to be the one to tell the Union guys they left Irving for dead if they did not pay. Leon agreed.

The two made their way to Imperial's cash room to organize the ransom. They counted out the money. Leon felt sick as he watched the stacks of bills disappear into a bag. As instructed, they did not contact the police.

The kidnapper told David to drop the money in a phone booth, near a Dunkin' Donuts, on Route 110, in Melville, Long Island, just a couple of minutes drive from the company plant. David then returned to the office. And they waited. Leon knew immediately that they had made a mistake. The rest of the day passed with no information. "Who the hell would be stupid enough to leave $150,000 cash in a phone booth," Leon ranted to himself and everyone around him. "We are idiots."

Days passed and they heard nothing. They tightened security at the company facility. No further threats were made. The money was gone. No one at the company claimed to know anything of Irving's whereabouts. Leon wasn't sure what to make of the situation.

Then, several weeks later, a call came from the police. A body had washed ashore on Staten Island, about thirty-miles from Imperial. They suspected it was Irving. The police needed someone to come to identify the body. David agreed to take on the grim task. When he arrived at the morgue, he found Irving's bloated, virtually unrecognizable corpse. Every bone in his seventy-something-year-old body had been broken.

It later came out that Irving's murder was a settling of an old score. He had double-crossed someone in a rival Mob faction, and his long-time protector had recently died, leaving Irving vulnerable. His murder apparently had nothing to do with his work at Imperial. Nevertheless, Leon and David continued to stay on high alert for several months after the incident.

Irving's disappearance brought an end to the constant Mafia shadow in Leon's life. As Leon poked around for more information, rumors percolated that Irving may have been considering putting out a *contract* on Leon's life, but the truth of those rumors was never verified. Leon never dwelled on the fact that he had potentially been in real danger. Instead, he rolled up his sleeves, and once again put all his energy into the growth and success of his company.

16

In the Twilight of the Twentieth Century

Imperial News Company expanded from magazine and paperback book distribution, to newspaper distribution in the late 1980s. In 1988, Leon acquired the rights to be the primary distributor of the *New York Times* and the *Daily News*. He created an enormously profitable spin-off company to handle the newspaper side of the business. Most of these multi-million dollar deals were executed with little more than a handshake. With the newspaper business, Leon had now created one of the largest distribution companies in the New York metropolitan area, and the money literally began pouring in.

Leon continued to work on the basis of trust and loyalty. His honesty was universally recognized in the publishing business, and continued to be one of his most important strategic assets. Even as his business grew, he remained hands-on, and kept a small-business approach. With literally millions of volumes of material to transport, Leon still poured over the numbers daily, retaining total control over the day-to-day operations of the business. Eliminating waste, and improving efficiency, continued to be his obsession, as it had been all those years ago in his one-room apartment in the Bronx. Leon was famous for working through his budgets, hand-calculating the numbers for the week, using the stub of a pencil as his only tool.

The old-world man, from the small village with no telephones, became one of the pioneers in the use of technology in his business. Leon, who was such a non-user of technology in his own personal life, that he, until the day he died, refused to leave a message on an answering machine, became one of the first in publishing distribution to envision how computers could revolutionize operations. Never interested in understanding computers himself, he invested significant amounts to purchase equipment and hire top programmers and technicians. He was able to automate the incredibly labor intensive and complex processes of driver route scheduling, billing functions, and order fulfillment systems.

Leon had been one of the early adopters of corporate computing, investing in an IBM 1440 that required an entire room to house the hardware. He proudly referred to his computer as his "baby." By the 1980s, his technology concepts were considered so advanced that the *New York Times*, along with other publishing wholesalers in non-competing markets, eagerly sought to purchase his custom-designed software. With child-like enthusiasm, he would consult with his chief programmer—laying out his ideas for automation and tracking, always amazed and delighted to see those ideas brought to fruition by the programmer. And yet, this architect of the most cutting-edge software barely knew how to turn a computer on himself.

Then, after almost thirty years of continued growth and success, Leon's instincts told him that the profitable days of publishing wholesaling were numbered. By 1988 the business was changing, and Leon saw a future where the publishers were looking for greater control, and would want to handle more, and more, of the distribution themselves. He had been correct in his predictions for the last three decades, and he convinced David that the time was right to sell Imperial News Company. Besides, Leon was seventy-two years old, and despite efforts to tutor some of his younger cousins in the business, there was no heir apparent equipped to succeed either him, or David.

They set a price of approximately thirty million dollars for the company. Several potential buyers were identified. An offer was made for close to the asking amount. Leon was advised by his accountants and his lawyers to accept the offer. He said no. "The number is thirty million dollars," he barked. "When they offer thirty million dollars, we have a deal."

His stubbornness infuriated his advisers. But within several months, as Leon predicted, they had a buyer. They got their asking price. Within three years, Leon watched with mixed emotions, as the new owner ran his once thriving, successful company into bankruptcy. Without the meticulous attention to detail, without the rigid oversight, without the trust and loyalty in the relationship with the publishers that had allowed Leon to negotiate rights to distribution based on nothing more than oral agreements, the business was worth nothing.

Leon retained the newspaper side of the distribution business for several years more. But by 1992, he and David had had enough of that, as well. David had become ill, and Leon, now almost seventy-seven years old, decided it was time to cash out.

He made his wishes perfectly clear to his accountants and his lawyers. He spent countless hours prepping them thoroughly for every possible nuance of the parameters of the deals, and then sat back silently, giving total control to his *lieutenants*, in the actual negotiations. The lawyers and accountants understood how Leon operated. They had garnered his total trust in the deal making. However, they also fully understood how unforgiving Leon could be; one screw-up, and they were out. Leon treated business like war. There were no second chances on the battlefields of World War II.

Unlike the sale of Imperial, the sale of the newspaper business also included the disposition of all assets, including the hugely valuable real estate assets that had appreciated many times over. His advisers encouraged Leon to compromise on some aspect of the complex deals that were being conducted; but Leon never budged. He had decided what was right, and what was fair, and he never second-guessed himself. Hundreds of millions of dollars passed hands in a series of all-cash deals, as the remaining distribution business, and the expansive real estate assets were sold. Leon calculated the numbers by hand. On one four million dollar real estate sale, he found a discrepancy of three cents in the closing statement, and was quick to point it out.

But when the months and months of negotiations were over, he realized he had sold much more than a business: he had sold a piece of his soul. His work was what kept him youthful, vigorous, and oblivious to the fact that he had slowly crept into chronological old age. At seventy-seven, he was still ruggedly handsome, youthful, and maintained his health, strength, and vitality. But all of that slowly changed.

He had few hobbies outside work, other than a passion for reading history, and enjoying the occasional chance to experience Russian culture through the Kirov Ballet, and other Russian imports to the New York City cultural scene. He and Betty had moved again—this time to an estate on Long Island's North Shore. They now had seven acres of land to oversee and a ten-thousand-square-foot home, a huge expanse of a house, that, save for just a few rooms, remained mostly empty. He had few friends, choosing to socialize with an increasingly insular group of Russian émigrés, people whom he had helped bring to the United States throughout the years, and whom he generously helped to set up economically. These "Russians," as Betty always referred to them, were in turn undyingly loyal to him as their patron. But it was an otherwise quiet existence. Without work to stimulate him, without the challenge of the next potential deal looming, Leon was bored, and he began to age.

With more money than he could ever need or spend, he continued to live his simple, even provincial, lifestyle. He still sat down to his favorite dinner of a homegrown tomato, a hunk of raw garlic, a slice of unbearably salty *schmaltz* herring, and some dark bread, all washed down with icy vodka. He tended to his plantings. He flirted with waitresses when they went out to eat. And he sat glued to the television in total disbelief as he watched the politics of the late twentieth century unfold, tears streaming down his cheeks, as the Berlin wall crumbled, the Soviet Union dissolved, Mikhail Gorbachev reversed seventy years of Communist rule, and Russian Jews could once again rediscover their

ethnicity, and their religious freedom. Always generous with his dona-
tions to various Jewish organizations, he now gave away millions of
dollars to the United Jewish Appeal, specifically to support efforts to
assist the immigration of Jews from formerly Communist countries.
All that he had lived through, all that he endured, all that he achieved,
had come full circle. Suddenly he was tired.

He was diagnosed with lung cancer in 1996. He had started smok-
ing during the war, and quit thirty years later; the damage had been
done. Doctors operated to remove a growth in September 1996. Over
the course of the next three years, he continued to struggle with the
cancer, and with debilitating emphysema.

By spring 1999, the cancer had spread. The radiation and chemo-
therapy treatments destroyed him, mentally, and physically. He was no
longer the man he had been fifty years before, the man who defied
adversity. Now he grew angry and defeatist, choosing to cloister himself in his private world, rarely going out, and only allowing visits from
a few chosen people. Betty tried to talk him out of what was clearly
depression, imploring him to remain in the world of the living. But he
stubbornly receded into his own world, refusing emotional help, and
viewing his illness as a sign of weakness of character.

In the early morning hours of August 10, 1999, just a few months
shy of the dawn of the new century, Leon Ajces died at home, in
Betty's arms. We were shocked. Even as he grew more, and more, ill,
we never believed that he would die.

Acknowledgements

I was so fortunate to have access to a number of people who generously shared their time, and their memories, to help me piece together the many incarnations of *Songa* into one coherent whole. Of course, first, and foremost, I thank my partner in this project, Betty Ajces. Quite simply, without Betty, this book could never have come to fruition. For her, the project was a bittersweet labor of love, to honor her late husband's memory and legacy. The rest of us benefit mightily from the lessons embedded in that legacy.

I am particularly indebted to those who dug deeply into their own painful pasts, as survivors, themselves, of one of the most horrific periods of modern human degradation. They informed and illuminated my perspective and my ability to tell Songa's story. In this vein, I thank Chana Goldenberg, Lola Amron, and Joseph Chekay.

Marilyn and Al Biegel proved invaluable to the telling of the story, and I thank them for their assistance, encouragement, and for providing me the opportunity to posthumously *interview* Marilyn's father, Herschel, via a videotape produced by the Shoah Visual History project. Leon Berkule paved the way for Songa's defection to America, and I thank him, both for his efforts fifty years ago, and for his retelling of those events today. Joseph Berechman, Penny Haberman, and Olga Dashevsky all represent the second generation of the survivors and descendants of Ozeryany, and the neighboring areas, and I am grateful for the stories they passed on to me.

I am indebted to Randolph Zander, formerly the senior civilian in the Eurasian Division of the Intelligence Group of the United States Army G2, in the late 1940s to early 1950s, who provided me with details, insight, and interpretation of remarkable clarity and accuracy, despite the fact that more than fifty years had elapsed since his interactions with Songa had taken place.

Boris Metter, Phyllis Leibowitz, Gerry Abraham, Joseph Walsh, Allan Weiner, and Steve Leavitt, all offered astute, and at times, humorous accounts of the man Songa came to be: a successful American businessman. I offer a special thank you to Russell Lewis, president of the New York Times Company, for his unique perspective on Songa, in his later years in business. A thank you goes out as well to Jackie Dashevsky, for her creative skills in designing the book-cover and photo section, and to my father, Professor William Green, for his assistance with the initial editing of the book. My mother, Marguerite Green, was the first person to read an early draft of the manuscript. Her enthusiastic response and encouragement gave me the personal ammunition to believe this project could be accomplished in a way that would meet the high standards she had ingrained in me.

My husband, Doug, supports me unfailingly in all that I pursue, both big and small, and I am truly grateful to have someone with such a uniquely unselfish soul as my partner in life.

Finally, for their continuous inspiration, I thank my daughters, Gabrielle and Alexandra, the children, of the children, of the children, of the refugees of Hitler's Germany. They are too young, now, to understand the content of this book. By the time they are old enough to understand, the last remaining survivors of that period of history will be all but gone. May this book help them to preserve memory, and to prevent ignorance.

About the Author

Natalie Green Giles, the niece of "Songa", spent her childhood and young adulthood captivated by his stories. A former management consultant with an M.B.A. from Yale University, she is now a freelance writer and a consultant, living in New York City, with her husband and two daughters.

0-595-65683-8

Printed in the United States
68555LVS00004B/31